Welcome Home, Davey

Determination kept me alive,
but it took love to heal the wounds.

Welcome Home, Davey

Dave Roever
and
Harold Fickett

WORD BOOKS
PUBLISHER
WACO, TEXAS

A DIVISION OF
WORD, INCORPORATED

Library of Congress Cataloging-in-Publication Data

Roever, Dave.
    Welcome home, Davey.

    1. Roever, Dave.   2. Evangelists—United States—
Biography.   I. Fickett, Harold.   II. Title.
BV3785.R63A3 1986   269'.2'0924   [B]   86–26636
ISBN 0–8499–0553–2   ISBN 0–8499–3111–8 (paperback)

Printed in the United States of America

89 80 1 2 3 9   RRD   9 8 7 6 5 4 3 2 1

With all my love
to
the two greatest women
of my life:
my mother and my wife

—Dave

Mornings I wake up early, way before the rest of the family. When we are on the road, which is most of the time now, my wife, Brenda, and I sleep in the master bedroom at the back of our Blue Bird bus. It's a big one, the kind entertainers travel in. About sunrise I awaken to find myself beside Brenda, everything much as it always is, but I always feel an element of pleasant surprise in her presence. After being severely wounded in Vietnam, one of the hardest things for me to accept was the depth of my lady's fidelity.

I often pull her to me in those first few moments of the new day. The warmth of her presence, the form and features of her being and the reality of our surviving relationship comforts my soul. I linger beside her, grateful that the recurrent nightmare I used to have never came true. In that dream I would come home to find the place empty, the loneliness growing into desolation. I would awake from that nightmare nauseated with anxiety and pull Brenda to me, desperate for consolation, as I do this day. I linger for another moment because the worst of the day is about to come. Then I rise and pad into the bathroom.

What I see in the mirror is the result of having been burned nearly to death. It isn't pretty. The right side of my face, my throat, and my chest down to the waistline have that streaked and melted look of skin grafts. My right eye is taped shut because the eyelid doesn't close naturally; so I have to tape it down at night, and frequently wipe it during the day, as it waters. I do not have a right ear. I am bald—this from the burns and simple aging. I pray for strength in everything else, but I do not pray for any grace that would block out the knowledge that comes from this daily confrontation with my grotesque image. This is the one thing I require of myself. I take responsibility for putting on the cosmetic appliances that allow me to go about in the world without causing so much head turning; although, of course, there will always be far more of that than I would like.

I untape my eye. I don my hair piece—a single one now which is superior to the two complementary ones I used to wear. I put on the plastic ear with fingers that refuse to straighten. As I do, my thoughts often trace the borderline between the will to live and despair. Sometimes I feel as though the real me has died; that's how much I long to reject my image as it appears to the world. Yet I do not pray for strength at this moment precisely because, in a sense, the person I used to be has died. My crewmates in Vietnam thought I had died and divided up the spoils of what I had left on this earth. My commanding officer wrote a letter to Brenda and my parents telling them of my death. But I have come back from the dead. And a man who comes back from the dead has a story to tell.

My father, Alfred Henderson Roever, Jr., started out in life as wild as could be. He lived on the Mexican border, smuggling pot into this country (they "blew smoke" in those days, too). At night, making his runs, he, the original hell's angel, would fly across the line on his big Harley-Davidson motorcycle.

He nearly died living that way. Out cruising one night just for kicks, drunk as a skunk, he rammed the Harley into the back of an old Mexican's donkey cart full of mesquite.

The cart had no tail lights and Dad never even saw it. He broke his leg, broke some ribs, and took a shaft of wood right up through his jaw and out his cheek. The front wheel of the bike was all bent out of shape, but—at least as I've heard him tell the story—he still pushed that thing a mile to get help. That accident really tore him up. His knees are still bad and his shoulder has given him trouble ever since.

Then he met my mother, Lois Matthews, a lady with a lot of class and a devout Christian. My dad was attracted to her, and she attracted him to the Lord. Through her witness, he made the strong personal commitment to Christ that he's lived by ever since. Mom was the chief influence in his life, as Brenda has been in mine.

My father may have been wild, but he was smart as a lick, and when he settled down with my mother, he trained himself as an engineer and started his own successful business as a contractor. He could build and fix just about anything. But later he went into the ministry, started preaching, and became the pastor of an Assembly of God church in Brownsville, Texas. There he began a long career as a pastor who started new churches, building both congregations and the buildings themselves from the ground up. He'd go into a town and get to know the local people, talk with the attendant at the gas station, the waitress at the cafe, the banker, the shopkeepers. He'd just go and make friends with them, and they would watch the way he lived. They'd sense the charismatic power and truth and trustworthiness of this man, and then he'd start up a small congregation.

I was born in McAllen, Texas, on October 27, 1946, while my dad was pastoring the church in Brownsville, Texas, right on the Mexican border. We lived there eight years, while Dad not only built his own church but traveled all over northern Mexico building up schools and churches there. Then we moved to Mission, Texas, for about five years until I was twelve or thirteen, and from there to Cuero, Texas. When I was sixteen, we moved to Fort Worth, where I met Brenda.

My father was a hard-charging man, tremendously demanding of himself. A gifted preacher who studied hard on his own, he was deeply loved by his congregations. His churches never wanted him to leave, but he believed his calling was to build strong churches, leave them in the hands of capable people, and then move on.

He was devoted to my mother. Every morning he would greet her at the breakfast table, brush her hair aside, kiss the back of her neck, and say, "Lois darling, I love you." He expressed his love for her openly in front of us kids, knowing how much it pleased her for us kids to know that he loved her. He was extremely courteous and trained his children to be so, too. My mother never opened a door for herself if he was with her, never had to pull up her chair, never had to hunt for her coat. I saw his love and devotion through his courtesy.

The work of the Holy Spirit was rich and deep in my father's congregations, but my papa never let anything get out of hand. The services were punctuated with a spontaneity that came from heavenly places; but they were orderly and decent at the same time. I remember the moments when the atmosphere got thick and I could sense the presence of the Lord. My heart was pounding fast; there was a tear in my eye, and I could feel something stirring inside me. I could sense the Lord's presence by the way my hair would stand up on my skin, and I'm talking about when I was just a little bitty kid.

We used to sing songs like "There is power in the blood, wonder-working power in the blood of the Lamb," and "There is a fountain filled with blood drawn from Immanuel's veins," accompanied by an old lady on the xylophone who could make that thing sing. When church was over and everybody was gone, I would go up there and pick up her little drumstick and pick out those songs myself, one note at a time, on the xylophone. At five years old, I could pick my way by memory through every song in the old songbook.

I was five when I first responded to God's call and sensed something of my destiny. You may doubt the Lord speaks to five-year-olds, but I'm telling you, it happened. We lived in a nice house in back of the church, nothing fancy or luxurious, but Dad always saw that we had decent accommodations. We ate in the large kitchen. I had a blue-green metal highchair with a lot of chips in the paint and little fold-out steps. I'd pull the steps out myself and crawl up into the chair. The two steps had corrugated rubber on the top, with a chunk missing out of the top step. I remember that highchair vividly because I always knelt at it while we prayed. We always prayed in the kitchen, kneeling on the floor, facing the backs of our chairs. I'd kneel at the bottom step and run my finger round and round the chunk of missing rubber on the top step. Then I'd put my head down on the top step and pray big time, you know.

After Sunday morning service, we'd go back to the house for a snack in the kitchen. It was after one of those spine-tingling services that I felt the Spirit move within me. The presence of Jesus had been so real to me even at the age of five that I wouldn't have batted an eye if someone had told me to scoot over so Jesus could sit down. After that service when my family knelt down around the kitchen table to pray, I put my head down on the top step of the highchair and started crying. I was not in trouble, I was not sick, I wasn't lonely, but I knew I was a sinner. And I knew that Jesus loved me when I wasn't worth being loved. When my turn came, I prayed that Jesus would come into my heart. While I was praying and crying I pressed my forehead hard against the corrugated rubber of the step, and I remember picking up my head and rubbing the bumps on my forehead where the rubber had left its impression. I'd feel those bumps while I was praying, and then I'd put my head down and make it bump up again. I remember praying and rubbing and crying and realizing deep in my heart for the first time that I was a sinner and Jesus loved me.

From that day on I knew I was going to grow up to be a preacher, an evangelist. When people would ask me what I wanted to be, I'd always say whatever occupation was big in my imagination at the time and then add on preacher: "I want to be a cowboy preacher" or "a fireman preacher."

As a little boy I loved to stand in the backyard and watch the garbage truck come down the alley. One of the big moments of the week was to watch that garbageman grab the big handle on the back of the truck that started the huge compacting mechanism. I wanted to pull that handle more than anything in the world. To have in my hands enormous power. To me that man was a kind of Samson, crushing the pillars of the Philistine theater, reducing it to rubble. At a very young age, I felt that a man's life had to have power in it. My daddy's did. And I came to understand from his means of working, the way he would gain people's confidence, that the condition of this power, as in the case of Samson, was righteousness, fidelity to the commands of God. If the people hadn't glimpsed a real spirituality in my dad's life those churches would never have been built.

So I associated the power I wanted with my daddy's mission—with being a preacher. And it seemed to me that the evangelists who so often visited my dad's churches had even a double portion of that power. These evangelists would stay right in our home and live with our family during revivals. I loved it. I was attracted by their independence, their knowledge of the world, their charismatic personalities, their personal sanctity, their charismatic power of persuasion. The evangelist has to be able to come in and adapt immediately to a particular setting. You don't have a year to get adjusted. You've got five minutes of the first service to win those folks' affections.

I loved to hear those guys talk, to hear them tell humorous stories to illustrate their points, to hear them preach the Word of God eloquently and persuasively. People speak of holding a crowd in the palm of your hand. You watch a good evangelist and you know what that means.

His every gesture brings into being and corresponds with what the crowd is feeling right then. Doing this, determining the thoughts and feelings of great crowds of people, under the anointing of God's Holy Spirit, was to me a mighty power indeed.

As I've said, the evangelists stayed in our home, and they were usually given my room. I was glad to make this small sacrifice. I'd return to my room after they left and feel as if I was moving back into a prophet's chamber—that my very bed was in some way anointed.

I think I felt my sense of destiny confirmed when, not long after I committed my five-year-old life to Christ at my kitchen chair, my dad ran over me with the car and I lived to tell about it. I was riding in the back seat of my dad's old Lincoln, of the vintage whose rear doors swung open from the front. I had recently had my first airplane ride in the little plane of a missionary pilot. The plane had a single stick control and I was fascinated by how this guy could control the plane with that stick.

In the back of that Lincoln, I started pretending that the door handle, which tilted away from me at a forty-five-degree angle, was an airplane control stick. I said, "Hey Daddy, I'm in an airplane," and pulled that handle. The door popped open and the wind blew it back. My arm was caught by the arm rest behind the door handle, and I was flipped right out of the car and knocked under the rear wheel. It ran over me from my right hip to my left shoulder; it left tread marks right across my chest and raised five or six long blood blisters. My head banged on the pavement and then banged up on the gas tank. I can still remember the sight of the differential and of the pea gravel in the pavement. I was rolled over a couple times, but finally came out from under the car and ended up sitting spread-eagle right on the divider line in the highway.

My dad was swerving all over the highway trying to stop. Cars behind me were taking off into the ditches to avoid running over me. Dad slid to a halt and came running back, just praying and crying and screaming, "Oh dear God, don't let him be hurt."

The people behind were screaming, "Don't pick him up. Don't pick him up." They were afraid I had broken bones.

He walked over and prayed and reached down and picked me up real carefully. I remember, as he held me gently in his arms, he prayed, "God, I will never forgive myself if this boy dies."

There wasn't a broken bone in my body, and not a scratch except for the blood blisters on my chest. When Dad asked me if I was okay, you know what I said? I said I thought I deserved some chocolate ice cream. The next memory I have is of sitting cross-legged in the middle of our big kitchen table, with Mother and Dad and my older brother and sister just staring at me, laughing and crying, while I dug away at a half-gallon carton of chocolate ice cream.

If my father embodied for me the power that comes through personal sanctity, my mother provided the chief image of the strength of Christ that can only be perfected in weakness. My mother was a brilliant woman, unusually educated for her time, a magnificent teacher, and always Dad's partner in running the churches. But I never saw her in good health. She had deterioration of the bone—her teeth fell out when she was nineteen, and her hip joint wore completely out at age sixty. She had asthma and emphysema—though not from smoking. She almost died at my birth. She had a benign tumor on the pituitary gland. It was treated by X-ray, which killed the gland as well as the tumor. She had to take artificial adrenaline and often lost control of her emotions. In her later years a stroke took away her speech, movement of her left side, and finally her life.

I remember coming home from school several times and finding her lying on the couch so still and so ashen that I thought she was dead. Scared half to death, I would walk over and touch her to see if she were alive. She would groan out a few words, unable to get enough oxygen. She had a breathing apparatus, called a Byrd machine, at home with her all the time. Many a night I heard the whirring and clicking of that machine in the back bedroom, and I would pound my pillow and try to curse God. "I hate You. If You loved her, You would heal her." It tore me up.

But then a few nights later I would hear the same woman in the back bedroom just singing her heart out in an ecstatic tongue of the Spirit. I would sit cross-legged on my bed, my head on my chest, and tell my dog—I had a puppy named Heinz 57 who slept with me all the time—"Dog, that woman is something." Then I would talk to God for a while and pray, "God, I didn't mean anything I said the other night. I didn't mean that. I just don't understand. But whatever she has now, I want that. I want to be able to sing in the dark."

Now and again I'd be hit with the fear that maybe Mama was sick because I had sin in my heart. I remember one time overhearing a conversation between my parents in which my dad remarked, "Since Davey was born, your health has never been right." He wasn't implying that Mama's illness was my fault, but I felt responsible.

Sometimes my dad would cry in my presence and say to me, "Davey, don't let your mama's sickness make you think that God doesn't love her or that He doesn't care about us. Know He is real." But then he would sob and say, "I don't know why God won't heal her."

Never once did I hear Mama blame God or express a word of doubt. Yet I do think there were times when she was deeply troubled in her spirit by her illness and wondered if somewhere she was wrong and that God wasn't healing her because He was punishing her. But she had learned not to let her emotions upset her faith in God's Word and His promises. She exhibited in her life how suffering can be a means of communing with God, a means of sharing in the sufferings of Christ, how through the honing of the spirit in suffering a man or woman can be sharpened for the use of God in a way he or she never dreamed of. One of my mother's favorite verses has become one of mine: "If we suffer, we shall also reign with him."

2

When we moved to Cuero I hit the painful and awkward stage of adolescence. I wanted so much to be popular, to exhibit the sort of charisma I admired in my evangelist heroes. My first attempts to gain acceptance failed utterly: I tried sports. I could be fiercely competitive, but I simply wasn't much of an athlete—the last guy picked and all of that. To top it all off, I racked up my back in junior high football.

So then I turned to misbehavior, as so many do, to attract attention. Smoking cigarettes seemed the fastest way to look like, and perhaps be, a real man. I just knew that if I could smoke I'd be cool. I went over to my friend Irvin's house one day and he was smoking. He was fourteen, his parents were divorced, and he was living with his grandmother who didn't seem to care what he did. That afternoon I smoked with him. When Mom and Dad came to pick me up, I smelled like a walking R. J. Reynolds factory. I got in the car and my mother said, "You smell like cigarettes."

Rather bluntly I said, "Well, it's probably because I've been smoking some."

Tears came to her eyes. She said, "Why do you feel like you want to smoke?"

"It's not that I want to. I think I'm destined to, Mom. Every family has to have a black sheep."

My mother had mastered the technique of a loving sarcasm or charitable irony that could both shame you and make you want to reform. She turned around and looked at me with this cynical little smile on her face which I'll never forget; she said, "Davey, there will be no black sheep in this family." That wry smile was as cutting and yet full of love as any smile I've ever seen. After that, I knew in a deep and searching way that to smoke would be to betray her.

Today many authorities stress that this sort of teenage rebellion is necessary in order to establish one's own sense of self. I'm told they call it "ego differentiation." I realize that grown men and women have to make their own decisions, but the feeling many adolescents have of being extensions of their parents isn't, to my mind, a bad thing. Those in a family belong to one another, and it's no use pretending that the actions of each member of a family don't affect the others. Parents serve, or ought to, as the conscience of the whole family, as Christ serves as the judge of His family, the church. Since the minds of both of my parents were enlightened by the light of Christ, they were an especially sure guide for my behavior. Even in rebellion I was secretly glad of the restraint my ties to them entailed.

Another avenue toward local fame was hot rodding. I was naturally gifted with mechanical stuff, and when I was fifteen I started building a car. I saved up my money from working at the H.E.B. grocery store and bought a '37 Ford pickup truck. I scrounged spare parts at junkyards, and my brother-in-law gave me a big Oldsmobile engine that I dropped in the thing. I built that engine up to be one hot machine. That little pickup would smoke tires and leave anything else in the dust. I liked the feeling of power it gave me in my hands and under my feet.

I started drag racing with other hot rodders from school out on an old black-topped country road. The same friend who taught me how to smoke was a little older than I was, and rather heavyset. I'd go get Irvin in my pickup because he gave me traction. I put him in the back end, and he'd hold that truck down. One day I tied Irvin in the back and then went out hot rodding this thing. I came over the hill just flying. The back end, I mean the whole thing, just lifted off the ground. The engine smoked because there was nothing on the wheels. I was off the ground. I looked back and Irvin's cheeks were half-way wrapped around his ears from the wind, and he was just hanging on for dear life, his big ol' belly sticking out.

Right then my steering wheel came off. It was a boat steering wheel that I thought looked cool. I'd beaten it on with a hammer. Being a kid, I hadn't cared if the splines matched or not, so it came off. I hit the brake, but I had only one—the front right. The truck spun when I came down because only the one wheel was catching. It shot me out in a field. All the while Irvin was screaming from the back. I pulled out about a hundred yards of barbed wire fence and finally I came to a stop after nearly bouncing to death over hard dirt that was corrugated like a washboard. Still I got my truck back on the road, tried to tie the fence back up, and came down that hill once again.

This time a highway patrolman was sitting there waiting on me. He got me, and got me good. He cited me for improper starting from a parked position (in other words, for "laying rubber"), speeding, no turn signals, no windshield wipers, no lights, no brakes, no exhaust system, no licensed driver in the front seat—I was on a learner's permit and Irvin was in the back end—and more. I can't remember all the charges.

Irvin of course found all this real funny, but I suddenly realized that this officer was going to take me to jail. All I could think about was my dad's ministry being ruined because his son gets thrown in jail. I looked at that officer and said, "Sir, my dad is a preacher and this is really going to hurt his ministry."

That guy unloaded on me. "*You* might have thought

about that before coming out here to terrorize the countryside. A preacher's son. The way you were driving that thing you were as likely to end up in a box as in that field over yonder."

I stayed quiet.

"A father who raises you up to know the straight and narrow, and a mother who loves you. Boy, I wouldn't have an ounce of pity for you—you are hellbent for leather, and it's fine with me if you end up there.

"But parents will love their children, *whatever* they're like. I'm going to see to it for their sakes that you stay on this earth a while longer."

I was honestly remorseful, and I guess he sensed that, so he let me off easy. But he made me promise that I'd park my truck. I agreed. He followed me home, made sure I was stopped completely, and told me if I ever took that machine out again before it was licensed and inspected, I was going to be in some kind of trouble.

Since I was no good at sports and couldn't drive my truck, I joined the band. I played the French horn and was even carted up from the junior high to play in the senior high band. But it was the guitar, which I took up about the same time, that proved to be my ticket to power and popularity.

By the time we moved to Fort Worth I was top-rated in Texas High School competition as a jazz guitarist. I could pick with the best of them, and the girls just swooned. I liked any song with a good long guitar riff in it; I'd make that baby scream for mercy, wail on that thing driving it to guitar ecstasy, and I remember some great late-night jam sessions with guys who loved music like I did.

I got my first band together in Cuero. We won the talent contest in our high school and began playing for school dances. My folks didn't know about that; to them, dancing was sin.

One of my playing buddies came from a talented family. His dad had a dance band that played for night clubs all over south Texas. We'd go to his house to practice. Jimmy would pass around cigarettes—which I would stick in the end of my guitar so it looked like I smoked even though I didn't—and break out his daddy's vodka. I'd let him pour me one, but I'd never drink it. I couldn't get it down my gullet. One day my folks sent my brother out looking for me, and he tracked me down at one of these practice sessions. There I was, a cigarette sticking out of my guitar and a bottle of vodka by my side, probably picking away on some provocative song like "Louie, Louie." He thought I'd gone to hell already. I wasn't even smoking or drinking, but I wanted so much to be accepted. I wanted to look like the rest of the band. On the one hand, I was selling out slowly but surely, selling my soul to be popular. On the other hand, I always seemed to be held in check by my sense of responsibility, by a fear of letting down those who loved me.

I remember one evening after the band had been practicing for a dance—I had told my parents I was studying my band lesson—when a guy said, "Let's go for a ride." He had been drinking the whole evening. As I drove by the Little League ball park, he yelled for me to stop, jumped out of my truck, disrobed, and streaked around the bases. I sat there saying to myself, *If a cop pulls up, I've ruined my life. I've ruined my dad's life.* I was just beginning to see the truth that "bad company corrupts good morals."

Another time it came out in the Sunday morning paper that I had played for a big Saturday night dance. As I was getting out of my hot rod in the church parking lot before the morning service, a big German woman named Sister Schoeber came up to me and said, "What is this I read in the paper that you played for a dance last night? Does your father know you play at dances?" I mean you could have poured gasoline on me and set me on fire and not have shocked me like she did. Admittedly, at the time my desire to play in the band outweighed my fear of letting down my parents, but I still felt a tremendous desire not to let down the people who loved me.

I can't omit the most important time my sense of responsibility kept me from shame. When I was fourteen I fell in love with a twelve-year-old girl named Annette. She was one of the prettiest girls I'd ever seen in my life, and I was absolutely infatuated with her. When the bell would ring at school, I would run clear to the other side of the building and up three flights of stairs just to wink at her and then dash back down to my room before being tardy. She returned my affection and one day, shortly before we moved to Fort Worth, when I was fifteen and she was fourteen, we ended up in a compromising situation.

But, moved by a force even stronger than sexual desire, I realized the mistake I was about to make. I had tears in my eyes, because I knew I shouldn't be there. It wasn't the girl I was worried about, and it wasn't myself; it was my parents. Suddenly, I saw my mother's face. Just the look in her eye, that sad wry smile, the same look that was in her eye when she saw I had been smoking. What would my dad have said from the pulpit? What would he have to compromise in his message if his son did what he was telling parents not to let their children do? God turned away from the Old Testament prophets who failed to bring up their children right. God might turn away from my family. However, the Holy Spirit interrupted my thoughts and actions so powerfully that it completely disspelled my passion. Thank God that no memory of compromise would have to haunt me.

That poor girl wondered what in the world she had done to squelch my advances. I never explained it to her. I wasn't man enough to explain that I was afraid I would hurt my parents. But I can say I was man enough to consider my parents more than my own passion at that moment. And I have been grateful ever since for the influence of my parents and for the sense of responsibility they instilled in me.

I went back to Cuero about ten years ago and held a revival in the little church. I looked around for my old buddies. Of the five who had been my closest friends, four were dead: one in Vietnam, one was hit by a car right on Main Street, one committed suicide, and one overdosed on drugs. If we had stayed in Cuero, I could have gone the same route. I didn't have the spiritual commitment back then to have held out for much longer. I hadn't outright rejected my childhood faith, but I was seeing how far I could compromise my family's values and still be a Christian. I had not yet walked down the aisle during a service in my dad's church to publicly confess my faith.

Part of the problem with Cuero had to do with how tough the street kids were and how hard it was to keep from becoming just as tough or suffer the consequences. I was never a fighter. I didn't like the jitters in my limbs, the racing of my heart that came when I got scared. There were Mexican gangs in Cuero, and, until I got my growth, they used to pick on me. They beat on me pretty bad a number of times as I was walking home from school. That alone made me scared enough that I had to hide from my parents until the tears stopped and I got control of myself. (In that irrational state I thought they might blame me for the trouble.) The worst of it was I always feared one of them would pull a knife and kill me. All I knew how to do in self-defense was sucker-punch, or sucker-kick, an attacker in the groin. After that I had exhausted my arsenal. I ran from fights and made friends with tough kids who protected me, avoiding confrontations in any way possible. These experiences stayed with me; and later on, when I joined the Navy, I was concerned that I might chicken out in combat. Bravery was not my middle name.

My mom and dad were concerned about me. They could see how the town was affecting me, even if they didn't know all the details of my behavior. I have a hunch that

Dad resigned from the church in Cuero and moved to Fort Worth in part to get me out of the element I was getting into. We were so poor that Dad asked me if I would sell my hot rod to help them pay for the move. He promised he'd get me another car as soon as we got our feet on the ground in Fort Worth.

3

My father went to pastor the Lake Worth Assembly of God Church in Fort Worth: a strong church, the largest he ever pastored, and about the only one he didn't build from the ground up. Soon after we got to Fort Worth, I met Brenda. She sang in the church choir. When I saw her that first Sunday, I was smitten, totally jazzed. Her jet black hair and the perfect features of her oval face made her beautiful, not merely pretty. The set of her eyes bespoke the Cherokee Indian heritage of her father. And when she looked at me with her steady gaze, I sensed a patient wisdom; I felt that this young woman could outwait time itself. One look at Brenda and I got over the girl in Cuero right quick.

Brenda's commitment to the Lord shone in her life. She was a living testimony to the beauty Christ can bring to a teenager's life.

I immediately began putting on the dog both at church and school, trying to act both cool and pious, but not fooling anybody, least of all Brenda.

My brother had the guts to ask her out for a date before I did. I invited another girl and doubled-up with them so I could make sure he didn't do anything with Brenda. My brother, after figuring out what was going on, managed in a gentlemanly way to swap dates so that I could take Brenda home. (The occasion, basically a group outing, allowed for his maneuvering without any hurt feelings.) I walked her to the door that night and tried to kiss her, but she wouldn't let me. I said, "I'd like to do this again sometime."

She said, "Well I'm not sure I would."

And *bam*, she closed the door.

I kept pestering her at school with notes. Finally, one day, standing together in the hallway, I told her I loved her. She slapped me across the face good and hard. She looked at me and said, "Don't you ever tell me that again," and started walking away. Then she turned around and added, "Until you mean it." That was the first intimation from her that I had a chance. But I knew I would have to prove that my intentions were honorable.

I had begun putting together a band when we got to Fort Worth, and we were soon being invited to play at dances and clubs. Once, when we played for a big school dance at the Ridgley Country Club, I sat with Brenda during the meal and asked her if she liked our music.

"No, I really didn't," she said.

I was crushed. I played the rest of the evening, but my heart wasn't in it. In fact, after the last song of the night, the entertainment coordinator for the country club came up to me and said, "Would you consider playing four hours a night on Friday and Saturday nights? I'll give you sixty dollars an hour." That was big bucks for us kids. With four of us in the band, we were talking a hundred and twenty dollars a weekend for each of us. But standing on the other side of him was Brenda. I looked at her, then back at him, and answered slowly, hardly believing my own words, "No sir, I'm going to be an evangelist." And I never played with a band again.

That same weekend I went to a special evangelistic meeting at my dad's church where the speaker was a young fellow named Audrey Holder, a protege of another evangelist, Laurell Akers. (Laurell Akers directed a summer camp which I attended for many summers and eventually worked at. He has had the deepest influence in my life other than my family.) The witness of Brenda's commitment had brought me to recognize the shallowness of my own faith.

Through this young evangelist, I could hear God reminding me of the calling I had felt as a child—of the vocation that had almost been silenced by the appeals of worldly success and power. That night I felt the desire for the reality of God in my life. I wanted to preach with anointed authority. I knelt and apologized to God for my lack of commitment. Then I got up off my knees and walked down the aisle. There was no thunder and lightning when I publicly committed my life to Christ, but when I walked down to the altar that night, I knew that my years of compromise were over.

Brenda was there. So were Mom and Dad. And what they witnessed that night was the biggest turning point in my life. We talked about it later that night. Mother cried for joy and my dad got teary-eyed. They made sure I knew that they knew what I had done. In so many words they were saying, *We're not going to forget this one. You've done something now that you made public, and you've done it at home among your own people and before your peers.* And, I added in my own mind, *before Brenda.* I knew that if she didn't believe in me and in the sincerity of my own commitment, she would never be my girl. I knew that I wouldn't be the man I was called to be, and the man she wanted, until I had given myself completely to Christ. That may sound like mixed motives, but I *wasn't* making a commitment to Christ to win the heart of a girl. My wish to be attractive to Brenda was one with my desire to be made attractive to Christ. My commitment to Brenda was proof to myself of the sincerity, not the fraudulence, of my commitment to Christ that night. And of my commitment to my vocation. Accepting my calling to the ministry was implicit in the decision.

In the course of one weekend I chose Brenda to be my wife (although it took a while to convince her), I chose Jesus to be my Lord, and I chose the ministry as my vocation, and

I've never looked back with any regret on the decisions I made.

After that weekend, the pieces of my life quickly fell into place. My last year in high school was my best year in every way. My grades shot up. I joined the Youth for Christ group and became president. My mentor, Laurell Akers, began letting me preach at youth camps. And, most important, Brenda began to show more interest in me. We started going out together more often, and she accepted my class ring. With her, even my sexual desires were reined in. If we got close, it was in her parents' home on the couch. The walls were thin and her folks were sleeping in an adjoining bedroom. We would hold hands tenderly but hardly more than that—there just wasn't any shame in our relationship at all. We'd watch television until the news went off, and then I'd go home. Our relationship developed slowly but surely as we grew more and more in love.

4

My mother and father encouraged me to go on to school, so I went to Southwestern Assemblies of God College, a Bible college, in Waxahachie, Texas, where I figured I could get training for my calling. The Bible college also seemed a good place to make contacts that would stand me in good stead later. My brother had become a French teacher there, after graduating from Rice University. I lived with him, in a little house-trailer in a park on the edge of campus, and got a job on the loading dock at a Sears store to pay my tuition. I worked hard, was soon promoted to dock supervisor, and began hiring on college buddies who needed jobs.

Feeling that the college lacked a liberal arts orientation, my brother made plans to leave his position after my first year at Southwestern. Not wanting to live alone—without family—I began to think seriously about asking Brenda to marry me. I had asked her once before, not long after we first started dating. When I thought of asking the same question again, I remembered how her slap had stung my cheek that first time. But we knew each other much better now, and I was fairly confident of success. So much so that I concocted a surprise as my way of putting the question to her once more.

I had the use then of a Grand Prix Pontiac, a big boat of a

car. It had bucket seats separated by a console. The only way for Brenda and me to sit close was for her to prop herself up on the console. Sitting there, she could lean her head against my shoulder, which she did that night as we drove out to a point overlooking a moonlit lake and the rim of lights on the opposite shore. When we got there we made small talk for a while, and I couldn't seem to angle in on the surprise. Finally I blurted out, "If you want what I've got, you've got to get off the console." What I had said might have meant anything, and she fell off the console from the shock of it.

When she opened the concealed compartment between us, she found the rings I had purchased and a bottle of Chanel No. 5 (I've given her a bottle of that fragrance at every important juncture in our marriage—anniversaries, Valentine's day, birthdays, whenever I get the chance. That stuff is "Love Potion No. 9" to me). I hadn't consulted her about the rings, something I later found she wished I had done, but she accepted them and the life together they symbolized. Actually, I'm glad I didn't consult her because she would have considered the stones I bought a shameful luxury. Today, she cherishes those rings and still wears them.

My father performed the ceremony on July 15, 1967. My brother was the best man, her sister the matron of honor; and we each had one other attendant. Standing at the front of the church, which was made to hold about two hundred fifty, I saw that it was packed; there must have been three hundred people there. Then Brenda appeared, in a white wedding gown with appliquéd roses—my lady and all the world to me.

The wedding party had decorated my Mustang with "Just Married," written in shoe polish, and cans and balloons as festive trailers. As we headed out, other motorists honked and waved, sharing our joy. We found as we drove that the groomsmen and their cohorts had played the usual tricks: our luggage had been stolen, and there was limburger cheese underneath the seats. We got our things back before driving on to Kerrville, Texas.

Kerrville is in the Hill Country of South Texas, the place where I had helped in the youth camps with Laurell Akers and still the most picturesque part of the country to me. They have the Natural Bridge Caverns there, better to my mind than the Carlsbad Caverns in New Mexico. Over the next few days we would spend some time walking and exploring. Really, though, we could have been in the most desolate section of God's earth, and it wouldn't have mattered much.

The thing was, we became lovers, and let me tell you, it was well worth the wait, well worth it. To take her into my arms and know that she was mine forever, to enjoy all the delights of intimacy—I was clean off my head. She was, too. God had made this garden of pleasure for us; He had tended it through the chastity of our courtship, and now we lived within it. We laughed and cried at the beauty of this new dimension of our relationship knowing that it was His special gift to us.

At the end of the summer, we moved to Waxahachie and lived rent-free in a nice house-trailer owned by some friends of the family. I landed a job at the huge General Dynamics plant in Fort Worth, and quickly worked my way up from washing company vehicles to collecting in-plant garbage, then to driving the tractor that pulled around the multi-million-dollar F-111 planes they built there.

I was still taking classes, but as my hours at the plant increased, my grades gradually dropped. Uncle Sam must have been checking grades, because when mine dropped below the minimum required to maintain my student exemption, I got my draft notice in the mail. My immediate reaction was to apply for a ministerial exemption. All I had to do was pick up the phone, call the district superintendent of the Assemblies of God, and say, "Rev. Anderson, I need an exemption letter for my draft board." I knew he would write it without batting an eye; he was a close friend of the family and knew my commitment to the ministry

was sincere. But—and that's the biggest "but" of my life—
my conscience got hold of me.

The next morning I was wakened by my alarm clock
radio. Still half asleep, I lay there, my mind putting pictures
to the news I was hearing. The announcer was detailing the
deaths of a group of marines in the DMZ that day. In my
dreamlike state, I wandered among the wounded. Although
I saw their suffering, I was unable to do anything about it. I
approached one soldier who was lying face down on the
ground. He was wearing his combat helmet, his weapon at
his side. He was bloody, injured or dying. Then I heard a
voice. "Why not me?" it said. "Why isn't that me?" I stooped
down and rolled the soldier over. And when I looked into
his face, I saw that he was me. I jerked awake, but I couldn't
shake that voice saying, "Why not me?" I can still hear it.

I'm sure it was my conscience saying to me, *Why weren't
you among those killed in the DMZ? What gives you the right to
be sleeping in this bed with your wife in your arms, living in a
comfortable house, while those guys are out suffering and dying
for your liberty?* I felt responsible for those guys.

When tragedy strikes, almost everyone asks, Why me? I
asked a different question, and the difference has deter-
mined not only my physical life but my spiritual life as
well. Not, Why me? but, Why *not* me? It wasn't a matter of
courage or any desire for glory. It related to the sense
of responsibility my parents had instilled in me; that in the
family of man, as in my personal family, we *are* our brothers' keepers; that we are responsible for what happens to
our neighbors, especially those who are innocent and suffering. What my parents taught me in essence was that
human life only becomes truly human in its ability to exhibit sacrificial love. Of course I couldn't have spelled it out
this way that morning—I could hardly remember my name
at that hour. But as I look back, I see how the context of
that semiconscious dream had been prepared through the
course of my life.

I couldn't ignore the voice of my conscience. I'm not sure how long I lay there in bed, but I finally looked at Brenda, woke her up, and said, "I'm going into the military."

Poor kid, she was stunned. She didn't cry or throw tantrums. She just said, "Are you sure that's what you want to do?"

"It's not what I want to do; it's what I have to do."

"What about the minister's exemption?" she asked.

"Am I a minister? I'm hoping to be one, but I'm not one yet." I rolled over and got out of bed. Later that morning I went down to the registrar's office to drop out of the semester that had recently begun—the spring semester of my second year. I enlisted on February 9, and by March 1, 1968, I began my training as a navy man.

My motives were mixed, to be sure. I was never a fighter, I had no desire to hurt anybody, I had a lifetime behind me of avoiding fights like a coward. I wanted to perform my duty to my country, but I did not want to go to Vietnam. I joined the navy because it sounded safer than duty in the other branches of the armed forces, and I figured it was a fair trade-off to put in the four years required of an enlisted man rather than the eighteen months or two years of the draftee who might get sent to the jungle.

Brenda and I lived with her parents in Fort Worth for the couple of weeks before I left for boot camp in San Diego. The night before I flew out, I didn't sleep at all. I just held Brenda close all night. I was frightened and had a lonely feeling in the pit of my stomach. I was second-guessing myself like crazy. *You fool, what are you doing? All you had to do was get a letter.* I was being unfair to Brenda. I had married her, taken her away, and here I was, bringing her back and leaving her with her mama. I didn't know where I was.

The morning came all too soon. We met the group of recruits at the airport and had no time for an intimate kiss

Dave and Brenda wed July 15, 1967. (Photo by Bill Rich)

Dave's parents, Rev. A. H. and Lois Roever.

Dave in basic training—
San Diego, California
March 28, 1968.

good-bye. Brenda was crying, but not sobbing. Our anxiety, of course, was over the ten weeks of separation during basic training. We never dreamed I'd be sent to Vietnam. We thought I'd pull time on a ship—that eventually the four years would be over and I'd come back home and we'd get on with our lives.

5

Between March 1968 and January 1969, when I shipped off to Vietnam, I underwent three phases of training: ten weeks of basic in San Diego, sixteen weeks of missile training at the Great Lakes Naval Training Center north of Chicago, and twelve weeks of special training for Vietnam river patrol duty.

Like most people, I remember basic training as a time of constant harassment and calculated humiliation. I was surprised, however, to find that I loved military discipline. I perform well when objectives are clearly defined and I can easily measure my accomplishments. If I know that there is a success level, and if it's clear to me what that level is, I try to achieve it. And in the highly structured world of the military, the next success level was always well defined. I was perhaps even more surprised to discover that I had a physical and mental toughness, which gave me an edge over my peers. I generally came out on top in the fierce competition. In fact, I was appointed master-at-arms of my training group, the position with commanding authority in the absence of the commanding officer.

We were given a variety of aptitude tests. They said I'd be real good as a missile technician. I agreed to go for further specialized training but, despite their sales pitch, I wouldn't agree to sign on for an extra two years.

All in all boot camp was a snap for me, except for the pain of being apart from Brenda. We weren't allowed to make phone calls, but Brenda and I wrote letters regularly. We didn't get any liberty until our last inspection, a couple of days before we were shipped out. I had no place to go, no friends in San Diego. All the guys went into town with sex on the brain and money in their pockets for the massage parlors, whore houses, and adult film cinemas. I didn't leave the barracks. I just stayed in and called up Brenda on the phone. Just hearing her voice about drove me wild.

During my ten days of leave at home I don't believe I was ever out of sight of Brenda. Every moment was a treasure of joy. We were so excited to be together again, our intimacy a means of communication that beggars all other languages.

For the missile training, married recruits were not required to live in barracks and could bring along their wives, although no money was provided for additional living expenses. But there was no way on God's earth I wasn't taking that girl with me to Chicago.

We had a hot little 1965 Mustang that I had bought when I was working for General Dynamics. We tossed everything we owned into a tiny U-Haul trailer and drove up to Chicago. We located a decent apartment in Kenosha, Wisconsin, not too far from the base, and then began church hunting. The next Sunday we went to the First Assembly of God Church of Kenosha, and were warmly welcomed by the pastor, John Wilkerson.

That very Sunday, after the evening service, Rev. Wilkerson asked us if we'd be interested in living rent-free in an old lake-side mansion the church owned. All we had to do in return was help fix up the place. We agreed as soon as we saw it: a once grand estate of years gone by, now pretty much in shambles but impressive nevertheless. Its sixteen rooms were arranged on two floors around a huge cathedral-ceiling living room. The spacious grounds had not had much attention, but the thoughtful design of the gardens was there to be discovered by anyone who could recognize the azalea bushes among the weeds obscuring them. There was a pier that stretched sixty feet out into crystal clear Silver Lake.

Brenda and I dolled that place up. We stripped and refinished the old hardwood floors, wallpapered and painted, and turned the basement into a recreation room for the church youth group. We earned our rent, but had fun doing it. It was an ideal situation for a couple of newly married kids. In retrospect, our months in the mansion on Silver Lake seem like an idyllic interlude in our marriage.

I remember driving home late at night after evening classes on our first anniversary. All the stores were closed, so I bought a cake from a cranky truck-stop waitress who cut it into pieces and made me pay full price for each piece. When I carried that cake in, Brenda was waiting for me, all decked out in fancy night clothes. I was totally in love with her, head-over-heels, gone man, gone. I set the cake on the table and pulled her into my arms. It was an evening we'll never forget. We decorated that place with rolls of toilet paper for streamers, put on music, ate cake, and partied into the night, two kids in love.

I worked on the house, but I studied hard, too. We'd typically have about five hour-and-a-half classes a day of highly technical training in missile mechanics and electronics. A lot of the guys just couldn't handle the material, but I applied myself and Brenda helped, drilling me at home.

I knew I was one of three or four at the top of our class of fifty, but I was still surprised when I was announced valedictorian, and, at graduation, seated on the platform right next to the admiral. It was the first time I had ever been the best. I was proud. And I was proud to have made Brenda proud.

Our joy was mixed, however, because only a few days before graduation we had received word that most of us would be sent to Vietnam. Before the officers said a word, we could see by the look on their faces that the news wasn't going to be good. A river patrol boat division in Vietnam had been nearly wiped out—90 percent casualties of both men and equipment—and our class was graduating at the right time to replace the division. The officers told us the story and said that they needed men for two duties: coastal patrol and river patrol. "We're letting you volunteer for the duty you prefer," he said with a certain Catch-22 logic, "because if you volunteer for something we know you will adapt more quickly."

The news really shook Brenda up, shook up both of us. For the first time I had to consider the possibility that I might get killed. Rationally, I knew there was a chance I would die, and yet spiritually I felt so sure of my vocation as an evangelist that I couldn't imagine God not bringing that calling into being. Then again, I understood the foolishness of presuming upon my hunches about God's good pleasure. I vacillated between fear and confidence, and got cold chills thinking about it.

I thought to myself, *Well, if they're going to send me, I'm going to volunteer and hope I get my choice.* I wanted coastal patrol because I felt like there was more space in the South China Sea than between the banks of a river in the jungle. River patrols had one of the highest death-rates among navy duties. But when I opened up my orders on graduation day, it said I was to report to the Naval Inshore Operations facility in Coronado, California, for special training in river patrol.

I couldn't take Brenda with me on this phase of my training. Wives weren't invited. And once again I moved our stuff and Brenda to her parents' home in Fort Worth. And although I was going to be training to fight and, if possible, survive guerrilla warfare, leaving Brenda for advanced training didn't seem that emotionally traumatic. I think we knew that the worst departure was ahead.

6

We were welcomed at the Coronado base as men with a mission. We were an elite group of guys, the cream of the crop, being trained for a highly dangerous job, and we were treated with respect.

Incredibly rigorous physical training began the first day there. By 6:00 A.M. we were out doing calisthenics, including deep knee bends and pushups until we dropped. And that was just warm-up. Then came our eight-mile run, in uniforms and heavy boots. The first day out was miserable; we stumbled, fell, cried, and crawled our way through those eight miles. Our platoon of about forty began together, but we were quickly spread out for miles, and nobody could keep up with the marine major leading us. He ran the whole eight miles backwards, egging us on, pushing us to the breaking point. Guys began throwing up, begging for mercy. Some guys just fell down, and everybody within hailing distance had to circle around and prod those who had collapsed into getting up and trudging on. The major wouldn't let any of us go on until that man got up and started running again. The intense peer pressure we were commanded to exert made us realize, after a while, how much our lives would depend on our buddies in combat.

We ran eight miles every day except Sunday. Our physical conditioning improved quickly. By the third or fourth day, I was able to stay up front with the leaders, partly because I couldn't stand to run behind the turkeys who would go out and drink beer and eat pizza at night and then throw up the next morning while running. The stench was enough to make *me* gag. We kept up a steady jogging pace, but toward the end the major would gradually start picking up the pace until he was sprinting the last half-mile, watching to see who could keep up with him. I had some trouble with asthma now and again, but I reached down inside myself for that last measure of resolve and motivation I didn't know was there. The running alone helped develop a tremendous sense of pride.

After cooling down from the run, we spent the rest of the day in intensive classroom training, beginning the first day with gruesomely realistic films of Vietnam river patrol duty. They showed boats blowing up, men injured, men dead. We had regular training in weapons, in radio transmission and code usage, but most of the training, both in film and lecture, concerned the operation of the boats we would be using.

The boats, called PBRs—a jumbled abbreviation for river patrol boats—were thirty feet long, and about twelve feet wide, powered by two, independently throttled, GMC V–6 turbo-charged diesel engines. The engines powered jacuzzi-type pumps, not propellers, to thrust the boat through the water—they were what water skiers call "jet" boats. The PBRs were made of fiberglass; they were light, maneuverable, and could fly. A small cabin, with steering wheel, two throttles, and radar screen stood behind a windshield about a third of the way back. About halfway back was mounted an M–60 machine gun. Underneath was a tiny hold, big enough for two people at most, where we kept the radio equipment, supplies, and ammunition. From there you could crawl through to the gun tub at the front of the boat, at the top of which—at deck level—were mounted two big .50–caliber anti-aircraft machine guns on a swiveling turret. Those guns were the chief artillery on the boat. Mounted on a tripod at the back of the boat, behind the engine-covers, was a single .50–caliber machine gun with a protective ceramic shield in front of the trigger. Each boat was operated by four men: one driving, one on the rear gun, one on the center gun, and the one in the gun tub manning the big guns up front.

Each crew member had a particular noncombat job, but everybody had to know everybody else's job. The boatswain was responsible for taking care of the boat itself; the engine man (or "snipe") took care of engines; the coxswain drove the boat; the gunner's mate maintained the guns.

Our duties would include carrying out the wounded, our own or those of the South Vietnamese—the Army of the Republic of Vietnam, or ARVN for short; we would "insert" specially trained guerrilla teams (SEALS), always at night, deep into enemy territory to perform highly covert operations, presumably CIA-sponsored assassinations and the like; we would draw fire to pinpoint enemy locations; we would even contribute to "public relations" by carrying in livestock, usually ducks, to civilian villages raided by the Vietcong. But the chief duty of the river patrol was to shut down the use of the waterways by the enemy. We would do this by engaging the enemy in boat-to-riverbank combat—called fire-fights—and by searching civilian rivercraft used by the Vietcong to transport equipment and personnel.

We were trained in how to call civilian boats alongside and then board them for inspection. *La day* meant "come alongside" and *concook* was the Vietnamese word for *identification*. Every citizen except children was to have an identification card with name and weight, date of birth, and hair and eye color. We were taught interrogation techniques, mainly how to respect the customs of the Vietnamese and remain polite. (Hand things with two hands; never point the soles of your feet at someone; don't throw food to the children.) We were given enough language training to ask elementary questions.

At Mare Island near San Francisco, where the swamp and delta land was much like the Vietnam terrain, we got hands-on boat experience. We learned how to maneuver those boats in every possible situation, how to dock, how not to get trapped in a narrow canal, how to make full-speed turns, how not to back up too fast. (They'll sink if you back them up too fast.) One night we were simulating towing a boat that had stalled on a mud bank. The rescue boat tied a strap to the back of the beached boat and began towing it backwards off the bank. But the rescue boat got to pulling backwards too fast; and the beached boat filled with water, and sank. For some reason, one of the crew on the beached boat—a tall, blond, real pleasant fellow— never got off and away. The rest of the crew swam off, but he must have tangled his foot in something. A simple exercise, but he drowned.

The Mare Island training was designed to simulate Vietnam duty as closely as possible and was plenty stressful. We'd be up three, four nights in a row with no sleep going through maneuvers just like the ones we'd be involved in during the war itself: load the boats, unload the boats, rearm, resupply, no sleep, combat rations, the works. Just when we'd collapsed on our bunks for a rest, the commanding officer would run in screaming, "Incoming rounds, incoming rounds, disperse the boats," and everybody had to jump up and scatter the boats.

The first time they started shooting blanks at us, without warning on nighttime maneuvers, I jumped out of my skin. Out of nowhere these incredibly bright flares came floating down on little parachutes. We were sitting there, suddenly in "broad daylight," and, man, I thought we were dead in the water. We had drifted right into their "ambush." Instantly there was a rat-a-tat-tat and flashes of gunfire coming from the riverbank. Boy, did we scramble. Of course, that's the whole point. They want you to say to yourself, *I've got to fight back or I'm going to die.* It worked, too. By the time I got to Vietnam the sound of gunfire was so common to me, those flashes in the dark so familiar, that when I finally heard the real thing, I never once felt like ducking and running. My only thought was that I had two seconds. If I didn't return fire in two seconds they would be on target and I was dead. But the instant I started returning fire, they had the same problem I did. They wanted to get it over with because they knew we enjoyed superior fire-power and maneuverability, and they didn't want to die, either.

While stationed at Mare Island, we were sent to Whidbey Island in Washington state, up near the Canadian border, for a week of the most difficult of all my military training. It was called SERE Training—the acronym stood for survival, evasion, resistance, and escape. We arrived in the morning and slept one night in reasonably nice barracks. But that was the last barracks we had. When we got there, our good uniforms and valuables were taken away. The only protection we had against the elements—and it got real cold at night—was our parachutes. We used them as tents. We were shown how to use a compass and how to read the topographical maps we were given. Then we, with no supplies or equipment, were taken into the woods, separated, and given three days to make our way to certain assigned coordinates, all the while evading capture by guys posing as Vietcong.

What they didn't tell us was that nobody would find his way out. Everybody would be captured and everybody would move from survival and evasion training to resistance and escape, or POW training. I'm proud to say, however, that because I was cautious, I was among the last to join the captured. I figured out where I was within a few hours by spotting a high point—a mountain peak in Canada near the U.S. border—then using the sun to find all

the coordinates. We were given no food whatsoever. If I had
been able to bring down a deer, I would have eaten it raw. I
ate some raw crab, which made me gag, and on six occasions I ate a slug—the same slug! My biggest source of food
was the soft green part underneath tree bark, the cambium.
I chewed that stuff all the time. It rained often, so there was
always water in the hollow of a tree or a rock to scoop out.

You could hear the enemy every now and then. The navy
used Japanese and Chinese Americans who had served in
Vietnam—some had been POWs in the Korean war—to
impersonate the North Vietnamese. They were dressed in
North Vietnamese uniforms, green with a red star on the
hat, and they were good at acting out their roles. They
spoke in broken English with a Vietnamese accent. Using
bullhorns they would yell, "Okay, you GI, okay, you in
trouble now, we going to get you boy. Where are you, boy,
you are going to be shot today." It made your heart pound to
hear them. The only time these Vietcong impersonators
dropped the mask and spoke in normal English was when
they spotted you and opened fire on you. Then they would
say in regular English, "You are wounded," or "You are
dead," or "You are captured." Or, if you overdid it in resistance, they would say in normal English, "They would kill
you." It was their way of saying, *We're breaking the program
long enough to let you know that you've fought back too hard
and would be killed for what you've just done.* And sometimes,
instead of even speaking, they used another code. If they
said, "Do thirteen pushups," it meant, *You've come close
enough that you might have been killed, but it's not worth
breaking the sequence of this program to use the queen's English
with you.* That's how technical, how realistic, it was. Those
were the rules of the game.

Once I heard a Vietcong guy tracking nearby. I saw him
before he saw me and I scampered to a big old tree. I was
just going to hide behind it, but I discovered that the whole
trunk was rotted out and I had enough room to stand in that
thing. I pulled some leaves up around my feet so I was

completely hidden. The guy walked by so close that I could have reached out and tripped him. He even sat down a minute before getting up and walking on.

Finally, they announced, "Okay, everybody who has not been captured, move down to the road at the lower part of the island." The North Vietnamese picked us up in a truck, even then treating us as though we had been stupid enough to get captured. They had weapons, but they didn't fire them. We had to get in the truck with our hands over our heads and squat down. Then resistance training began. Our resistance took psychological, not physical, forms. In the truck, for instance, when they told us to do anything, none of us obeyed their orders. That was resistance. We'd also stared straight ahead, no matter what they did. Show that jaw, throw that shoulder back: that was resistance. Another means of resistance was for all of us to shuffle our feet, raising a ruckus and kicking up dust.

We were in the jungle solo for three days. Then we were kept in a compound which simulated a POW camp. When we got to the POW camp, we were stripped naked. They ran us through showers (not as part of the punishment, actually, but to clean us up after living in the wild for days). They gave us no food. No housing. We were kept in the compound on our feet almost all night. We would sit down and lean up against each other and try to sleep. We were kept in a pen out in the open, surrounded by chain-link fence about twenty feet high with razor-wire on top. We did have water; there was never a shortage of water.

We were issued old tattered and torn clothes with no fly zippers or buttons. Then they would come up and say, "You GI, you button up, you button up your coat, where your button?" Then they would slap us around because we didn't button our coats. That kind of abuse took place continually, hour after hour, day after day.

They had black canvas bags that they would dip in water and put over our heads and tie tightly around our necks. No matter how hard I tried, I couldn't get air through that bag. I would start suffocating. My heart would get to flut-tering, I'd get real dizzy, and I would start to lose control of my bladder. Finally terror itself took possession. I'd think, *They're going to kill me.*

Then they'd jerk the bag off and say, "What's your mama's name, tell me your mama's name."

I wanted to say, "My mother's name is Lois M. Matthews. I'll tell you anything if you won't put that bag over my head again."

Yet I knew that when they pulled that bag off I had to resist. So every time they pulled the bag off, I would grin. But everything in me wanted to scream, *Please don't do it again.* And I knew that because I grinned he would do it again. But that was what resistance was all about.

He would put the bag over me again until I would almost black out, then he would jerk the bag off. They knew exactly how far to go. "Tell me your mama's name, what your mama's name?"

I would stand there and just grin.

I must have endured the canvas bag a dozen times. They were doing their best to break me. When the guy pulled the bag off the last time and I was still grinning, he put the bag back over my head and hit me right in the face. He must have doubled-up his fist and hit me as hard as he could across my nose and mouth, because my bottom tooth came right through my bottom lip. The blood spurted out. When the guy pulled the bag off, I looked at him and said, "Do thirteen pushups." He had gone too far. I knew it and he knew it. This was training. They were to push us to the edge of psychological breakdown and capitulation, but they were not to deprive the military of a soldier by inflicting injuries that would take time to heal. When I said, "Do thirteen pushups," he walked off. I never saw the guy again. I think they pulled him out of the program. I don't know why he overdid it. The drama in which we were all engaged may have become too real for him as well.

Some guys did break. They put us in small pine boxes like

baby coffins—too short for an adult to lie down in. Four or five guys would push you down until you were sitting with your legs flat and your head pushed down almost to your knees. Then they would hammer the lid down and walk off and leave you. After a while our tormentors returned. They beat on the coffins with sticks as hard as they could—you can't imagine the noise in that box. Intermittently, they pried off the lid. They grabbed you by the hair and pulled you to a standing position. I had no feeling in my legs. I felt like I had been amputated from the navel down. When they let go I collapsed like a bean-bag. They pulled me back up again and again until feeling started returning to my legs and I was able to stand there all wobbly legged. Right when I gained some measure of control I was shoved back down in that coffin. I almost lost it, man. The only thing that kept me quiet, kept me calm, was quoting Scripture.

The coffin was too much for one guy; he went into a psychotic state of what psychologists call "infantile regression." I heard him screaming and crying, "Oh mama, I want out, Mama, Mama. Tell them to let me out. Mama, please. Mama. Mama."

They also put us in little interrogation rooms with bright red lights. Those rooms felt evil, as though they were after your soul, as though you would be tormented by demons. There, they told us every ungodly, filthy thing they could about the presidents of the United States. They told us that these men loved pornography, that they were whoremongers. I'm sure the same sort of brainwashing tactics were used in the real POW camps, techniques used to demoralize you. The point, of course, was that if presidents cannot be faithful to their wives, then how can they expect you to be faithful to your country, to deny your own will to live when they cannot control their physical appetites? All ethics proceed from basic commitments of fidelity: friendship, marriage, patriotism, even Christianity itself depends on obedience to vows that structure our conduct. The North Vietnamese sought to undermine our basic commitment as soldiers to uphold our oaths to defend America, to *demoralize* us, to the point that we would be willing finally to stand in front of a camera and denounce America. The training experience, of course, was to teach us how not to be taken in.

The use of sex to demoralize us was the shrewdest strategy the enemy could have chosen, especially in the context of Vietnam. Sex was a tender subject to the GI. The enemy of course knew this. If the sexual improprieties of beloved presidents were revealed, then the GI, who was constantly trying to live down his own sexual immoralities, could justify his own sin and guilt by saying, "Well, fat on America. I'm not going to die so that my commander in chief can live a life of immorality."

Remember, at this time the sexual revolution was just starting to take off. Most Americans had not yet accepted its amorality. So even though Vietnam was one long orgy for a lot of the GIs, they still had at least some guilty conscience about it. If that could be destroyed or effaced, if fidelity had no hold on any part of a person's life, then a whole new sense of self, a basic change in the way we think of our identities, could take place. We'd no longer see ourselves as supernatural creatures made in the image of God, who are therefore responsible to God for the vows we keep or break; we'd no longer be men with souls, but complicated animals distinguished only by the variety of our needs and appetites. The brainwashing was all designed to get us to think of ourselves as animals—just animals with appetites for food, drink, sex—because then we could shed our ideals like so much dead skin.

The hardest stress to bear came when they started punishing another man because of you. Claustrophobia, fear of drowning, fear of darkness, fear of suffocation, all these things were bad enough. But when they put you in a no-win situation, which entailed guilt whatever choice you made, the psychological pressure really got bad.

Those who impersonated the North Vietnamese watched

to see which guys buddied up and drew moral support from one another. One fellow and I, for instance, encouraged each other. I don't even remember his name now; he was a short, stocky, well-built guy with round glasses and sandy hair. They took us into a room where a guard was sitting at a table eating a bowl of steaming rice with chopsticks. We had not had a bite of cooked food for a week.

This guy looked up and said, "Oh, very good, very good you are here today. You two boys doing very good." And he started talking to us in the most pleasant way. "Would you like some rice?" In walked some guy with two bowls of rice. "Here, you sit here, you eat." I stood there looking at that rice and, man, it smelled good. But my partner looked at me and we walked over and spat in the rice.

The guy looked at us and said, "You should not do that. You eat, you eat," and he held it up so we could smell it. We spat in it again.

I said to myself, "If he holds it up to me again, I'm going to knock it out of his hand." I figured if I did, they would probably say "Too far" because they would have to clean up the mess, right? But he just set it down and left it there the whole time.

We are ready to accommodate you, he still implied, *if you will accommodate us. You help me and I will help you.* That's what it amounted to.

I answered his every question with, "Milton David Roever, B728361, 27 October, 1946, U.S. Navy." I wouldn't give him the time of day.

Finally he said, "Okay, against the wall." So we backed up against the wall. He pointed to my partner and said, "Put your head on the wall." Then he pointed at me and said, "You tell me your mother's name." Every time I wouldn't respond, my partner was forced to take a step forward while keeping his head against the wall. Finally my partner was at about a 45-degree angle, keeping his body stiff. Oh, the incredible strain of trying to hold that position. His whole body began shaking all over from the muscle spasms. The interrogator kept screaming at me, "Tell me your mother's name. Don't make your friend hurt. Look what you're doing to your friend. It's your fault." My buddy said nothing. He was in so much pain tears were running out of his eyes. Finally he fell. He had suffered as much as he had the strength to withstand and I hadn't said a word.

In my presence the interrogator said to my partner, "You remember your friend. He no love you, he not like you. You die, okay, him not die, you die. He let you die before he tell anything." Talk about guilt! When we got out, I whispered to my buddy, "I'm sorry, man, I'm sorry."

Another time they squashed me with another man, a lieutenant, into a vertical box about the size of an outhouse for about sixteen hours. We were forced to stand face to face, forehead to forehead, nose to nose. All we could do was force our heads off each other so we didn't breathe in each other's face. We urinated in our pants.

One man, a lieutenant colonel, succumbed to his hunger. Ironically, he had made it to the last two hours of the whole thing. We were all lined up and they brought in a big round black kettle, about four feet across. We watched them bring in huge chunks of fresh meat. They threw in the meat, they threw in whole potatoes, tomatoes, cabbage heads, lettuce heads. Then they filled the kettle with water, and cooked that big stew on an open fire right in front of us. Oh, how good that stew smelled! We could hardly stand it.

Tears came to my eyes. We thought they were preparing it because the program was almost over. There was enough in that one kettle to feed everybody. I talked to several of the guys and said, "I think it's about over and they are going to give us something to eat." When the food was ready, the men posing as enemy guards walked up and asked us if we were ready to speak to the cameras, or something to that effect. When nobody agreed, they all walked over, unzipped their pants, and urinated in the stew. I can't describe how I felt—watching them do that.

Then they overturned the entire kettle, dumping all those roasts and vegetables out on the dirt.

Next, they brought out baskets of fresh fruit and said, "Are you ready to talk now?" That's when the lieutenant colonel lost it. The guard walked over to this fellow and held an orange right in front of him. The poor guy reached for it. I'm glad I happened to see it, because it taught me how fragile the human mind can be. The guard pulled his hand back and threw that orange high up against the chain-link fence, where it stuck about twelve feet off the ground. The colonel took off running and screaming, and crawled up the fence after that orange. They pulled him out of the program immediately. They carried the rest of the fruit off, but that one orange stayed up in the fence, tempting us all.

Then suddenly we heard machine-gun fire from out of the bush. Rat-a-tat-tat, bam, bam. I mean it was realistic. The gate swung wide open and in came U.S. troops, clothed in full uniform and carrying American guns. We had gotten used to seeing only communist weapons, AK–47s. The North Vietnamese flag flying over that place came down fast. When the GIs pulled the flag down, we attacked it. We shredded that flag until there was nothing left but threads. Then they raised the American flag and a bugler started playing "Battle Hymn of the Republic." I bawled, I was so happy. We all cried and hollered and hugged each other. It was over. We had succeeded. Oh man, what a feeling. It made me love America as I had never loved America before. It was like I had actually been a POW; that's how good our captors were at their job.

You should have seen us after we were liberated. After we went back to the barracks to clean up, they bused us to this big cafeteria and said, "You guys can order anything you want." It was real early in the morning and everybody wanted breakfast.

I am not kidding you, I ate at least a dozen eggs and a huge mound of bacon. I drank orange juice and milk until my stomach ached.

You can guess what happened. I went out and threw up. When you have gone that long without eating, you have to be careful. You have to eat light things like soup and crackers. You have to come off that thing slowly and carefully. But our gorging was still worth it. We went back in and ate more. It was a fiasco, but we loved it. I get goose bumps just remembering how everybody would laugh and cry and poke fun at each other; we felt a camaraderie like you never dreamed. That's what the training was all about: teaching you to survive, teaching you to resist and escape—all that's great; but it also established among those guys bonds of an indissoluble fidelity.

I was so glad that I would go to Vietnam with a sense of purpose, a sense of team. Vietnam was a unique experience for guys who were involved in the kind of training we went through. We would have died for each other. Even though the men I trained with were dispersed throughout Vietnam, I joined other guys who had gone through the same kind of rigorous training, and we felt the same spirit of unity.

I was amazed at what my navy training did for my confidence. As a boy, I didn't have it. As a boy, I felt as if I couldn't win, I couldn't do this, I couldn't do that. It wasn't until the military, when I was forced to compete against other men, that I found out I was no wimp. My daddy had raised a winner. In a way that those other boys' fathers hadn't, my daddy had put in me the strength that only comes from obedience. Graduating first in my class, surviving the POW training, not breaking under the pressure, not getting captured, all boosted my confidence tremendously—and that confidence later helped hold me together when the rest of my life was falling apart. The training did its job. It really got to the spirit and soul of a man.

After river patrol training I had a ten-day leave before my departure for Vietnam. Before I flew to Fort Worth I called Brenda and asked her to come by herself to meet me. After weeks of separation, I longed for an intimate reunion. So, we made plans to spend time alone before seeing the rest of the family. I am not ashamed to say how much I needed her love and affection. I had seen the sexual license and infidelity of other guys, and I knew that I had something better. I didn't have a bad conscience about my strong physical desire for my own spouse. Brenda was my beloved wife, a woman who would wait faithfully for me in my absence. I never for a second wondered if some guy was successfully putting the make on her while I was gone. It never even entered my mind. I trusted her completely, and her trustworthiness helped me remain loyal myself.

Meeting Brenda at the airport turned out to be the closest I ever came to enacting the fantasy I later dwelled upon in Vietnam: I envisioned myself coming home from the war healthy and fit, stepping off the airplane to a welcome home party of two, just Brenda and me. Then off we'd drive to our honeymoon paradise—alone together at last.

On the other hand, I couldn't quite put out of my mind the sound of bullets and the fact that they soon would be real. Our intimate times were precious and full of joy, but we also cried a lot. For ten days we had red eyes. And it wasn't just being scared for myself; it was fearing that Brenda might be a widow.

We talked about raising a family. One day, sitting in the Mustang I said, "I don't know what's going to happen to me. I don't know if I should leave you pregnant so that, if I don't come back, a part of Dave Roever would still be on this earth. Or if we should hope for the best—and wait. If you have a baby while I'm gone, you might have to raise it alone." We finally agreed that, for the child's sake, we ought to wait until I returned.

I still count saying good-bye to Brenda as the most painful moment of my life. If I had been going over as a chopper mechanic, we would have had a party. But I knew that I had a good chance of getting killed. After all, we were replacing a division 90 percent of which had been wiped out. I knew that I might never kiss her again, never kiss those lips that so comforted my soul.

I flew out of Love Field in Dallas, and, on the drive to the airport, I don't think we said a word. Brenda's parents and my parents rode with us. Her parents were weeping. Her dad, wonderful old guy, was trying not to, but couldn't stop the sniffles. We prayed together in the car before we walked into the terminal. Our family always prayed—over everything.

I was taking a commercial flight to San Francisco and there were no other military personnel at the airport; in fact, the airport was mostly deserted of civilians as well. Wearing my dress blues, I looked sharp. I was in magnificent condition, about 190 pounds, not an ounce of fat, six feet tall, twenty-one years old. I told my mother, "Mom, I love you." I didn't say anything to my dad, just shook his hand. Nothing said as much to my daddy as looking him straight in the eye. Don't blink, don't look down, don't look at his nose, look him in the eyeballs. And I did. He gave me no instructions, no final words. I don't believe he could have spoken. I know my daddy too well. I recall his steady gaze in return, the look in his eyes that communicated his steadfast love and loyalty, a look that filled me with courage.

During the final moments before boarding, our folks backed away to leave Brenda and me alone. I kissed her and held her. I held the back of her head up, pushing her face hard against mine. Her tears were hot, her cheeks feverish and flushed. The tears made her lips taste salty. I felt her mouth trembling. She was trying not to cry.

That moment haunts me. I was a strong man. I was a healthy man. I could look in the mirror and know that I was normal. But I left that. And there are times today when I become angry because I left it all. I get so tired of children staring and parents peeking rather than looking, and I want to say, "Hold it, you come here and hear the whole story. Sit down and in ten hours I am going to pour your ears full. These scars are gold; this discolored face and disfigured body are war decorations and gold medals to me. I don't like being pitied or humiliated. You are going to hear it all."

I confess it still hurts to remember that day I kissed my beloved good-bye because she never again saw her husband the way she married him. Never. She never saw me like that again. The man she married, the man she kissed good-bye, never came back.

When I had to go, the lump in my throat cut short my breath. It hurt to speak. The memories are too much for me sometimes. I said to her, "Baby"—these are the exact words—"Baby, I'll be back without a scar." What a thing to say. It was as though I knew what was coming and made my first joke about it to deflect someone's pity. And when I kissed her—that last peck on the cheek—and turned around and walked off, I could have died.

I walked onto that commercial airplane and sat in a seat, surrounded by civilians. Nobody cared that sitting by them was a guy going off to what would probably be his death. They just drank their booze, smoked their cigarettes, and read their *Time* magazines, while I sat there trembling, scared, thinking, *God, I'm never going to see her again.* I wanted to cry. I wanted to throw my arms around a total stranger and say, "Please hold me. Don't let me go." I sat there, and I wished I could get off the plane.

Yet I didn't lose it, I kept it together. I ordered some coffee. I was trying to learn to drink it because "good military men" always drank coffee. I never even told the man beside me where I was going. I never said a word to him. I didn't read anything; I didn't even look out the window. I just looked at the back of the seat in front of me until we landed in San Francisco. I was numb. And I wasn't thinking of Vietnam. I was thinking of her. I was thinking of the salty taste in my mouth. I tasted it for eight months. I remembered how soft her lips were. I think that's one of the reasons I kiss them so much even now. I kiss her all the time. I hold her all night, even now.

We flew to Vietnam on a 707 contracted by the military but owned and serviced by Pan Am. From the West coast we flew to Hawaii where we refueled. We got off and poked around in the airport a bit—I bought a postcard—but the other shops were closed and it was dark outside. By then I was fairly stable emotionally. I had dozed off on the plane, and when I awoke I had gotten myself in gear mentally. Our next stop was Guam, where I talked on the phone with a friend, Carl Allbaugh. He was a captain in the air force, a navigator on a B–52, who flew bomb raids over Vietnam. I told him I was on my way to Nam and he prayed for me on the phone. I got back on the plane and we flew into Saigon.

There had been a lot of partying on board. The stewardesses wore provocative miniskirts and showed off their fancy ruffled underpants. I was glad I had been home with Brenda. I focused my thoughts on the beauty of our marriage rather than the scene before me. That was just the beginning of the sexual indulgence that marked the

58

atmosphere of Vietnam for the American GI. Those stewardesses were trying to show everybody a good time. They had everybody laughing and high. Liquor flowed like you wouldn't believe. The guys drank and played card games until the people holding aces passed out. Everyone knew there were soldiers on board who would come home in plastic bags. The mentality on the plane was "Eat, drink, and be merry for tomorrow you die."

We circled high over Saigon until we got clearance to land. Then that plane dropped in like a rock because they couldn't make long approaches. Being seated up front, I was among the first to get off. When the big door opened, the heat and odors of the place hit me like a slap in the face: the smell of burning engine fuel, much like kerosene; the musty smell I came to associate with Vietnam itself; and what I took to be the smell of decomposing bodies. The first thing I noticed were the bullet-shaped, brushed aluminum coffins stacked beside the runway to be shipped home. Welcome to Vietnam.

Then several old school buses, painted blue with big screens over the windows, pulled up, took us over to customs, and then bused us into downtown Saigon to the dilapidated old French hotel where we stayed for three days of orientation. We unloaded just as a big USO show was packing up to leave. Here were more American girls all dressed as sexy as they could be. Sex on the way over. Sex when we arrived. Everything seemed to center on sex over there. That's all the guys talked about, that's all they dreamed of, that's what they spent their money on. It was as though they were going to Vietnam for the biggest, longest orgy of their lives and they could hardly wait to get there.

We spent three days in Saigon. The first day we were all lined up in the shabby hotel ballroom to receive orders for our duty. My orders were to Riverboat Division 573 stationed at Sa Dec. Then we received a series of briefings mainly on surviving noncombat life in Vietnam: how to keep our weapons from being stolen, how to avoid being the target of terrorist and pickpocket activity, how to avoid contracting VD and what, in graphic detail, would happen to our bodies if we did. We weren't issued our combat uniforms, boots, gear, and our weapon until the third day. We didn't get any ammunition until we reached our point of assignment. My combat uniform had the distinctive "tiger green" camouflage of the naval special forces: long horizontal streaks on a slightly darker green base. We had a lot of free time the second and third days to wander around the city.

Traces of Saigon's former beauty as a French colonial capital made the pervasive atmosphere of dilapidation and decay all the more depressing. The streets were littered with trash and jammed with oil-splattered cars; there were lots of rickshaws and little Fiat taxis which were painted royal blue and canary yellow. The city struck me as a seedier version of Bourbon Street in New Orleans: French architecture, mansard roofs, and windowed doors opening onto small balconies. Little kids, even some lepers, wandered the streets or sat and begged. Others laid out their wares to sell on the sidewalk. The American presence was everywhere, not only in the military but in the modern, Western modes of dress and behavior that the Vietnamese people themselves were trying to adopt. The young women wore tight Western jeans and halter tops. They ratted their hair into bouffant styles. All the music—on the streets, in the cities, in the barracks, even on patrol—was Western rock. You seldom heard Vietnamese music in Vietnam. It was as though Americans were trying to create a back-home atmosphere by surrounding themselves with the trappings of Western culture, but somehow the back-home moral responsibility got lost in the transition.

I remember taking a picture of a telephone pole on a street corner in Saigon that must have had three hundred power and telephone lines connected in chaos and gobs of wire just hanging down off of it. That telephone pole symbolized my impression of a city heartlessly jerry-rigged and patched together, demoralized and debilitated by a sense of impending doom, of modern technology showing its helplessness against the darkness in the heart of man.

Saigon struck me as a city of uncontrolled passions, as a city whose moral guard was down, indeed, as a city outside the pale of morality. The guys were reaching out for the girls—and prostitutes were always within reach—almost as soon as they got off the bus. I said to myself, *What will those guys be like when this thing is over? Whatever they may have done at home, God knows what they are going to do here.*

The war didn't come to Saigon that often, yet. It was still mostly jungle warfare. Occasionally incoming rounds hit here and there and the enemy penetrated where the GIs' defenses were weak: in the brothels where guys would get their throats cut and in the bars where occasionally the door would swing open and some guy would lob a grenade into the crowd. But in one sense the *real* war was fought in the bars and brothels of Saigon because it was there that many men sold their souls. Saigon was in a war zone all right: the war zone of the soul.

We spent three days in Saigon. I never was in the city again until my injuries took me there for preliminary treatment on my way home.

9

My orders were to Sa Dec. First I took a troop carrier airplane to the Air Force base at Can Tho. There I boarded a Bell Ranger helicopter which took me to the base at Sa Dec, about forty-five minutes away. I remember the strange sight of the terrain as we headed across the jungle. The earth took on the appearance of a tropical moonscape with crater holes everywhere from the bombs dropped by the B–52s. The craters had filled with water and from the air they looked like stock ponds. They reflected the blue sky and clouds, flashing white as the sun hit them from our vantage point. These crater ponds stood out vividly in the thick, dense jungle. As we started our descent, I felt the tension among the crew. Everybody had his eyes peeled and the gunners fingered their triggers.

Two officers were waiting for me when I hopped out of the chopper, dragging my sea bag behind me. They shook my hand, grabbed my bag, and welcomed me warmly, mispronouncing my name, as people often do, as "Rover" instead of "Reever." While we drove to the compound in their jeep, they filled me in about the base, about my coming to the best river division in the navy—all the typical hype.

The compound at Sa Dec housed about 150 people— personnel for the boat base and the SEAL team. The boats were docked on the river about half a mile outside the compound. Inside the compound, there were bunkers everywhere—just pits with sand bags stacked up waist-high with gun-mounts built in. Guards were posted in the corner bunkers. Traffic flowed through a wide yard between a round-top Quonset hut that housed base headquarters and the big two-story barracks—a wood, canvas, and screen structure, open from one end to the other. The walls of the barracks went up only to about eye-level, with an open gap between the top of the wall and the roof so that air could circulate over the walls. It still looked hot to me, but I soon learned that everybody had an electric fan to push along the breeze that came through the screens. The toilet and shower facilities were in another building.

Except for the sleeping barracks, the buildings were air conditioned. (I spent a lot of time in the cool library.) But the only place to get a cold drink—even milk—was the base bar.

Sa Dec was a sharp little compound. When I got there I was issued sheets, pillow cases, and blankets, and assigned a bunk. Ammunition for our machine guns was issued from the boats. I carried only six or eight clips—with about a dozen rounds per clip. I slept with that gun.

When I walked into the barracks, I was surprised to see some of the guys had their own little concessions. They were real entrepreneurs, selling booze, electronic gadgetry, trinkets which passed as local art, and memorabilia of the war itself.

Every bunk had a personality all its own. The guys made their bunks homey by putting up pictures and posters: photos of the family or of the girl at home. I remember a lot of Rolling Stones posters, Beatles posters, and peace symbol posters. The GIs who brandished the peace symbols often seemed to be the most violent. They lived out a paradox fundamental to the war. They claimed they didn't want to be fighting; but bang, bang, bang— they loved the action, the "rush" it gave them. They were addicted to the adrenalin-high of combat, and they lived for their fix. A lot of those guys didn't want to go home; some were in their third and fourth years of combat duty, which meant that they had repeatedly chosen to stay.

I never put up any posters. The only personal touch around my bunk was one picture of Brenda. I carried no pictures on my person either. I even took off my wedding ring and carefully stored it, along with other valuables, in the toe of one of my old boots. If I were captured, the enemy could try to use knowledge about my family to manipulate me.

That first day, I was introduced to my commanding officer and my team—there were eight of us in all, four crew members on two boats which always patrolled together. My CO was Lieutenant Rambo. (His name is no joke; I suppose Sylvester Stallone's Rambo is just pure coincidence.) Rambo was an outstanding man, very capable and responsible. He was probably thirty-five years old and gutsy as they come. (The CO was in charge of the division, not the base, so when Division 573 pulled out of Sa Dec, another group came in with another CO.)

After I got moved in, we went down to see the boats. I could hardly wait to get on board because that was what I was there to do: to get on that boat. Each eight-man group was transported down to the dock area in the back of one of the big green U.S. Navy trucks with tires that had that big knobby tread. The road down to the docks was cobblestone.

Docked on the river were not only our boats but the flat hollow cargo barges where supplies and ammunition were warehoused. The barges, made of thick protective steel, were tied together in rows out from the dock. Ten patrol boats docked down there, two for each of five crew teams. There were no names on the boats, no numbers, no identification of any kind. This prevented the Vietcong from taking revenge on any particular boat.

I started going out on patrol with my two-boat, eight-man team as soon as I arrived at Sa Dec. I remember inspecting some boats on my first day out, learning the ropes from my boat captain, who reminded me how to look for weapons, what to ask, what to watch out for—that sort of thing. We inspected boats every day, unless we knew we were going in to provoke a fire-fight with the enemy.

The Vietnamese rivercraft we inspected were usually old wooden vessels ranging in size from small sanpans to huge multi-carrier junks, as big as small tankers. Searching one of those large junks was often an all-day job. Anytime we saw a craft with a suspicious air about it, we had to stop and search it. And there were a million places on those vessels to hide stuff. We had to look behind everything, never knowing when we would reach into something and have our heads blown off. It was scary, especially when we were poking around down in some dark, cramped hold.

We looked for hidden passages on the big water tankers, doors that wouldn't open. We had to poke long poles down through holds filled with rice to feel for anything solid that would indicate caches of weapons or ammunition. We checked out the clothing of people, including hats. (The scene in the movie *Apocalypse Now*—of the woman throwing her booby-trapped hat into a helicopter and blowing the machine apart—is utterly realistic.)

I learned by experience that a favorite Vietcong hiding place for grenades and ammunition was in the big pottery canisters used to transport a foul and pungent-smelling sauce used for seasoning and made from decomposing fish. The fish for the sauce were processed at factories that you could smell miles away if the wind was right. They knew that Americans were generally revolted by the smell of that stuff, and that we weren't about to stick our hands down into the canisters. Wash all you want, your hands stunk for a week. But I got real brave about scooping my hand into that sauce.

I wanted to smell like a Vietnamese and have the sense of smell of a Vietnamese. I noticed that the indigenous people, living in a society without deodorants and artificial scents, had a much keener sense of smell than the average American. I think the Vietcong often detected the presence of Americans by the scent of shaving cream or cologne. I took to washing my clothes by towing them behind the boat and strictly avoiding any scent other than plain soap.

Our biggest problems came in searching the water taxis—twenty or forty feet long, some as long as sixty feet, with big old noisy diesel engines creating a din—packed with passengers. You get some guy in there who is a VC and he blends in with the crowd. Crammed together in close quarters, a guy can easily pull a knife and stab you. And the awkward M–16 is no protection at all. I even developed a modified weapon for just such situations. I took an M–1, cut the back stock off, made a pistol grip, and cut the front barrel off just in front of the slide. I taped three banana clips together and attached them for my front stock. So I had a highly maneuverable automatic weapon not more than ten inches in length.

Usually we used an interpreter to interrogate, often one of the civilian policemen whose uniforms consisted of a white hat, white shirt, and blue pants, which won them the nickname "white mice." More than once we found that our "white mouse" was Vietcong. He would pretend to help us interrogate during the day and then shoot at us at night. My distrust of the white mice motivated me to learn the language myself. (The old woman I hired for a time to do my laundry helped me with the language.)

I remember noticing something one of these guys said that made me suspicious, but I let it pass. That night he stole every weapon off the boat that wasn't tied down: three M–16s, two grenade launchers, and three pistols.

We brought along a white mouse only if we were pretty sure we would have to do interrogations that day. Basically most searches required simple questions: "Have you seen the Vietcong here? What makes you think they're here? How do you know they're here?"

The guys on my team seemed real young to me, but of course I was hardly any older. They were interesting, loyal fellows, and we worked pretty well together. Our captain, the first of three I would have, drank all the time. He was naturally friendly, and had the most pleasant smile. We liked each other but were not close friends. We didn't share stuff that was private or confidential. But he was the guy I liked to sit with when we ate or relaxed—the guy I liked to laugh and cut up with.

The snipe and rear gunner, whom I eventually nick-named Pervert Number Two, was the youngest of the guys, a year-and-a-half younger than myself. He was a stocky-shouldered Texan, and was my best friend over there. He was really a quiet-natured guy with a good sense of humor, but our lifestyles were quite different. A couple of times I think what I stood for must have pricked his conscience.

Our midgunner, in charge of the boat, was a tall, skinny California boy. He had a good sense of humor but our moral standards were miles apart.

A few days after I arrived, our team was part of a big armada—sixteen boats, if I recall—that headed up to flush out and take over Devil's Hole, the name we gave to an island criss-crossed by man-made canals, in the center of which was a village rife with VC activity. Ours was the lead boat, and I was the front gunner; the first man to pass by Devil's Hole was me, a rookie. There was tremendous excitement in the compound when orders came down that we were going into Devil's Hole. It was known to be a communist stronghold. Reconnaissance had recently spotted evidence of a major build-up of supplies, ammunition, and personnel in there. Our commanding officer warned us to expect heavy resistance. The plan, he explained, was to try to pull the Vietcong into a confrontation so we could let them see what they were up against. It was no secret ambush operation. We knew they were there, and they knew we were coming.

They opened fire on us right away. The bank of the river

seemed to streak towards us as the tracers of light weaponry flashed. The enemy had some heavier artillery, but not much. They were relying on the usual AK–47 machine guns plus a few rocket-propelled grenades and B–40 rockets. (We found these weapons later during the body count.) One of our boats took a hit but nobody was killed. We were the ones with the heavy artillery, and we pounded those banks like you wouldn't believe. When we got through, there was no one left firing; anyone who had lived had retreated.

In a fire-fight like that, you don't see people, you just see the tracer bullets from the automatic weapons, and you fire back to the source of that tracer. You go for it, man, and you just pump your own tracers in there. You just keep pumping; and all the while you're begging, *Please, God, don't let them take my head off.* You pump for everything you're worth, because the more you fire, the more they duck into their trenches. The more they duck, the less they aim. The less they aim, the better your chances of coming back alive.

When we were out on patrol, it was almost a relief when they opened fire; the suspense was almost more frightening than the action. When the enemy had shown his location along the riverbank, then we would start making our firing runs: open up the throttle and head up river to the top of the firing zone, then circle back down along the other side to the bottom of the firing zone, then back up through again. You just keep circling until it's over or you're out of ammunition. Most everybody screams and hollers, exploding with tremendous rage. I can't repeat much of what they yelled, but I certainly understood the life threating pressure of the moment.

I usually didn't say anything. I had one thing on my mind: keeping my guns on the enemy. When we would come back down along the firing zone, the wake of one of the boats going the opposite direction would cause our boat to slap—whomp, whomp—up and down. There was no way to keep my guns absolutely steady, and I would see tracers taking off in all directions. I would be saying to myself, *Boy, I hope I don't hit the wrong people.* I had to really work to keep those guns level. As I got more experienced, I could sense the next rhythmical slap of the boat on the water and move my guns up and down accordingly. My two guns fired five hundred rounds a minute each, so I was putting a thousand rounds a minute of .50–caliber bullets into those banks. Every fifth bullet was a tracer with a little white phosphorous charge on the back of it, so that when the bullet was fired I could see its direction of travel.

After a fire-fight, like the one that day at Devil's Hole, we beached our boats and went in to flush out and inspect all the bunkers along the riverbank. Anybody still alive was captured. Seeing the bodies always made me sick at heart. One question always haunted me: Did I kill that guy in the bunker? The one who must have been running away because he got it in the back? Did I kill any of the dead?

We left the bodies, but took our prisoners back to base in our boats. After receiving medical attention they were turned over to the South Vietnamese forces for interrogation. I think I can say that the Army of the Republic of Vietnam (ARVN) often killed their prisoners. One time in particular I remember seeing a man floating dead in the river whom we had turned in the day before.

Checking out the bunkers after a fire-fight had its own peculiar stress. You never knew exactly what you'd find. On the day of the big battle in Devil's Hole, for instance, we took in a Russian woman journalist, armed with a small-caliber pistol. She was ushered out real fast. The brass knew they had a prize, and they didn't want her hurt. They didn't want an international incident either, I'm sure.

Time after time I stood in front of an open bunker carefully aiming a shoulder-fired rocket at a soldier who came walking out with his hands on top of his head. We'd been warned that if the slightest thing out of the ordinary happened, we were to fire a round into the bunker. The VC knew that was what we'd do, so they cooperated.

I found no heroes among the North Vietnamese. They always gave up. They would often come out saying *"chou Hoi,"* indicating they were renouncing their homeland. There was a program to relocate these expatriats in the South, which included inducements of amnesty and property on which they could live. Those who screamed *"chou Hoi"* were not only surrendering, but surrendering to become part of the Republic of South Vietnam. I know some of those guys fought just to be captured so they could get free property. Few were willing to risk themselves in combat. Most of the time they would stand in a bunker, hold a gun over their head, and open fire without even aiming.

I know all the stories about how young the VC soldiers were, how we were fighting children; but, honestly, I never saw any children soldiers. Most of the Vietcong I saw were in their mid-twenties or older—older, that is, than most of us. And most were North Vietnamese, the Vietcong "freedom fighters" were few and far between. But then I only dealt with one aspect of the war. I know ground soldiers who did encounter true believers among the VC, men who were both young and heroic. But I think my experience gave me a better sense of the enemy in general.

So after we'd flushed out the bunkers and taken prisoners, we went back for the body count. We'd roll over the bodies, then look through their clothing for identification documents. We collected any relevant material we found in the bunkers: weapons, ammunition, and so forth.

The conflicting emotions were draining. After a firefight, I'd be elated that I was still alive, and sick at the sight of the casualties. To some of the GIs it all seemed like a game for which they'd take trophies; they wanted to cut off ears of the enemy dead, that sort of thing. There was clearly more restraint if we were in a large group. In a small group, say one team of eight men, anything was possible.

When we got back to the barracks after the raid on Devil's Hole, a lot of the guys went straight to the bar and got stoned—standard operating procedure for many of them. My values didn't allow me the luxury of anesthetizing the pain. I went straight to my bunk, put my face in my pillow, and cried and cried and cried. I kept saying, "For God and country, for God and country, for God and country." That was all I said, over and over, until I cried myself to sleep. But that was the last time I cried. I became callous, too.

I didn't have booze to take away the pain of events like the big fire-fight at Sa Dec, but fortunately I had a more effective pain-killer for the desperate fear and loneliness of war: Brenda's letters, tape-recorded messages, and the packages she sent stuffed with goodies.

The packages arrived twice a month. I had a virtual addiction to Fritos and bean dip, and she always included these in the treasure trove in the middle of the packages. She also sent candy bars, gum, and cookies. The fragile items were insulated with popcorn. My buddies really went after that popcorn; an unwritten law about treats from home decreed that everyone shared something—you shared or suffered being an outcast or worse. Anyway, I was always left with the best of the provender and tore into it for the sweetness it gave, the taste of Brenda's kindness.

The tape-recorded messages arrived more often, maybe once weekly. At first we had little reel-to-reel recorders, but the speed settings were different and distorted the sound. We soon had cassette players and that improved the quality of the tapes. Hearing someone's voice, sitting there out in the jungle, you can't imagine how much closer it brings her. I would sit right down and listen to the tape in the barracks, with an earphone if others were around, but I preferred the resonance of the regular speaker.

I always listened and responded immediately, finding somewhere to be alone. Sometimes I talked to her as if we were lying in bed together, pretending that it had been a normal, long, hard day, and now we were lying there in the dark, speaking openly and without urgency as couples do who savor the last minutes together before dropping off to sleep. Then I often reminisced about our days together. And I always ended my messages to Brenda by contemplating returning from Vietnam and being alone with her in our own home. That fantasy and those weekly tapes kept the closeness of our relationship very much alive. Hearing Brenda's voice regularly, helped bring sanity to the seemingly insane world in which I was living.

I never talked about the details of the war. Brenda knew enough to realize the danger I was in without my driving her crazy with frightening details. I wanted to share these things with the one I loved, but it was that love which kept me from it.

Brenda also wrote to me every day—every night to be exact, right before going to bed. She scented her letters with Chanel No. 5. For her part she never asked me questions, like how to get the car fixed, which gave me the least bit of evidence that she was having trouble coping with her life.

She was working at Sears and living with her parents. These settings provided the context of her simple letters. She told me every benign detail of her day, the chicken she had prepared for dinner, her new blouse, a movie she had attended. I was always elated by her letters. They all began in the same way, "I love you, I miss you, I want you." The last statement meant most of all because if she didn't still want me she could hardly love me with the strength necessary for her to remain faithful. A beautiful woman her age would have opportunities to cheat, but her repetition of those lines let me sense the strength of her loyalty.

There were times, the loneliness of the war being so bad, that I might have deserted given half a chance—but how do you hitchhike out of a jungle to San Diego? What I'm saying is that without her letters I believe I truly could have gone crazy.

The imagination, though, can be a powerful defense when used right. I would take every detail in those letters and use them to transport myself mentally back home. I sat at the table where they ate that meal Brenda had prepared, I drove with her to work, I attended church and Sunday school with her. Her letters filled me with an enthusiasm for living again because they allowed me to block out the war and pour myself into all those things which make life worthwhile. Brenda told me later that my letters always made her cry; they reminded her how precarious our future life had become. I might have reacted that way except that my meditations on home were so intense that for hours in my daydreams *I was at home.* The war became the unreal thing. Those letters, tapes, and packages kept me going; I wouldn't have been able to bear the war without them.

About three months into my tour of duty I found out the date of my first R and R. It was to take place five days after our anniversary. I collected all the brochures I could find and decided on Hawaii. Brenda was so excited she started packing that day. From that time we had an extra hedge against the difficulties of the war; we could tell ourselves, "Well, four months, (three, two, and so on), then we will be together again."

We started to allow ourselves to look toward the future in other ways. As I've already said, we decided not to conceive a child while I was in training, but now that I was in Vietnam, we started discussing names for our future babies. We also considered what ports I should put in for after my tour in Vietnam—I would have two more years left to serve once I left combat behind.

It was my love for Brenda that sustained me in Vietnam. Without her, I'm not sure I would have been able to bear the loneliness and horror of war.

Our boat was relatively new and in good condition. Our snipe was the best, and he enjoyed his job; he liked working on those diesel engines so much that when we had time on our hands—running errands like taking in beer to an army outpost, or delivering mail which took the boat captain away for a few hours—our snipe would pop the covers off those engines and tune them until they were purring like a kitten.

The boats took a lot of punishment. Whenever we got back from a patrol we would count the bullet holes in the hull. Those were our trophies. "Look how many rounds we took! Woe, Roever look at this. You almost lost your family life, man." AK–47 shells could go through the fiberglass hull of the boat, but not the aluminum of the gunwale. Grenades would of course have done considerable damage, but we were generally too far from the bank for the VC to throw a grenade at us. And it's hard to hit a moving target. You can heave a grenade about as far as you can lob a baseball. But whenever those boats were really moving, you were not going to hit them.

I remember one nighttime patrol when we had cut the engines and were drifting down the river, trying not to make a sound. I was pushing us off the bank with a long pole so that brush along the bank wouldn't screak down the side of the boat. All of a sudden I heard a splash right next to the boat, and a couple seconds later a grenade went off underwater. The boat lurched and the water spouted straight up about twenty feet in the air. The sucker who had thrown that thing had missed from only a few feet away. Incredible. I unloaded at the bank of that river. I probably dumped a thousand rounds on that sucker. I knew he was in there and that made me mad. Here I was just minding my own business, and he almost killed me. Just inches.

We all wore flack jackets, always. They were hot and miserable but we wore them. They weren't going to stop a bullet, but they could slow it down enough that it wouldn't do as much damage. They could stop flack, hence their name. We always wore helmets out on patrol. Just the helmet, the flack jacket, and that was it. It was so hot I would often peel off my clothes and wear only my underwear under the flack jacket. I fought many a fire-fight standing behind those guns in my skivvies.

The rear guns had a protective ceramic shield, but the front guns were unprotected. The guns themselves provided the only shield for the front gunner. The guy up front was thus the most vulnerable, but he has the most power: two anti-aircraft .50–caliber machine guns are something to contend with. The guns I manned were dual-mounted on a rotating turret with an electronic, not manual, trigger mechanism. You could use one trigger to fire them both, but their firing rates were independent.

When I would fire, the whole boat would vibrate in sync with those guns. After a long round of firing, the barrels would glow cherry red down by the chamber. They were incredibly noisy. But you couldn't plug your ears because you've got to be able to listen, and when the enemy starts firing, you don't take time to put plugs in your ears. I'd be nearly deaf for twelve hours after a fire-fight.

My guns were mounted about shoulder-high when I stood between them down in the gun tub—which was a little more than waist deep—and I sighted through a crossed circle mounted between the two guns. They were aimed very slightly inwards, so that they would actually cross-fire at about five hundred yards. A manual crank on the left side spun the guns around. But really all I would do was to give the crank a turn to get the guns moving and then throw my shoulder into the gun and those babies would spin real fast. The ammunition belts fed into the sides of the guns from a can underneath. They didn't get tangled because the ammunition belts were coiled in boxes on the pivoting turret and thus they allowed free movement.

I was welcomed and accepted by the rest of the men at Sa Dec. Nobody ever made me feel like a rookie. The closest thing to an initiation rite was when you got to cut a notch in the little looped ribbon hanging down the back of your beret after your first fire-fight.

After I'd been out on patrol a few weeks, I saw what was in the heart of some of the GIs. Devil's Hole may have been the name of a place, but it was also a condition of hate that unsettled me.

Our boats kept returning to Devil's Hole looking for VC movement on the canals near the village. Now, there was a general curfew in Vietnam. Nobody was supposed to be out after dark. Of course if we went up the canal and sat there, nobody came out, and we didn't catch any Vietcong. So what we did was to cruise up to the village and nonchalantly throw some garbage overboard. But hidden in that garbage was a real sensitive microphone, a hydrophone, attached to a thin, strong wire.

We had probably two miles of that wire rolled up on a huge spool hidden in the back of the boat. The microphone sunk to the bottom of the river, only about ten feet deep. Then we slowly cruised back down the canal, playing out the wire as we went, and dropped anchor at the edge of the island. The wire measured very accurately how far away we were from the microphone, which we had dropped at an intersection of two important canals. We anchored there the rest of the afternoon and waited for night to come. Then we turned on the amplifier on our end of the wire and could listen in on what that microphone was picking up.

Sure enough, around 11:00 P.M. we began hearing the click, click, click of little boat engines crossing the canal. Every time we would hear a boat, we would launch a mortar shell, judging the range by measuring the wire. Those people couldn't figure out how in the world we could hear them crossing. One time we must have scored a direct hit and blown a boat right out of the water, because the next morning there were boat splinters floating all over. We assumed that any activity was VC. Nobody was supposed to be out after curfew, and our job was to enforce the curfew, to stop the Vietcong activity in Devil's Hole.

Early one morning while curfew was still in effect, even though the sun was coming up pretty good, we picked up a boat on the microphone. We dropped a mortar in. Bang. A few minutes later, here comes a little sanpan out of there with a young woman and an old man in it. This little boat pulls up alongside and the young woman—she looked maybe eighteen or twenty—was rattling away in Vietnamese. We looked down at the old man sitting there, holding his ankle, shaking all over. He looked like he must have been eighty years old. We could see a smooth hole clean through his heel. You could see bone, but he wasn't bleeding at all. The last mortar we had fired must have sent a piece of shrapnel right through the old man's heel. The young woman was real upset. I felt sorry for her. The old man was pale and in shock.

I brought him on board and said we ought to take him in for medical attention. Everybody agreed. But when we had laid him out, one of our guys starting imitating him, twitching and shaking, and laughing. To see this kind of callousness in my teammate made me sick.

Hatred for the enemy could really bring out the evil in a man's soul. On another occasion I saw it happen to a company sniper, an expert marksman who was issued a fabulous weapon. Being a sniper was his chief job, although when he wasn't on a sniper mission, he was a gunner on a PBR. I have good reason to believe that he opened fire on a water taxi and sank it. He was one of those guys who loved the war.

I wish I could forget the day we came in from patrol and saw something lying on the pier. As we got closer I could see it was a human body. Then I realized it was a young woman, seventeen or eighteen, maybe younger, definitely a teenager. She was in traditional black garb—black pants with flaps front and back down to dress length and a white blouse. She had black hair, pretty complexion—and bullet holes all through her. I was stunned. She was lying there sprawled out on the dock, the sun baking down on her dead body. Nobody else around. *What in the world?* I thought. *Where had she come from?* I hollered at the guy who refuels the boats, and he came out of his little shack and said, "It's Larry's (not his real name) trophy."

"What do you mean 'Larry's trophy'?"

He said, "He shot her today."

It was as if she were a deer and he had shot her and thrown her body up on his car to show it off to the boys.

Then Larry himself came up, beaming. He went over and kicked her leg this way and that saying some rather foul things. I was overwhelmed with a disgust and rage like I'd never known before. Fighting hard to control myself, I looked at him and asked, "Why did you kill her?"

He said, "I told her to *'la day'* and she didn't." *La day,* again, is the Vietnamese expression you use when you want to order a boat to come alongside to inspect it.

If a boat didn't respond, we were to fire an M–16 tracer over the bow. But Larry must have opened up immediately without further question or warning. Her multiple wounds were not from one tracer bullet, but were clearly from automatic arms fire. I highly doubted she was VC. If she had been, Larry and his crew should have found weapons or documents or other evidence which would have been displayed as prominently as his "trophy." To my knowledge, nothing was ever said to him about it.

That scene left one of the deepest scars of the war on my heart. No wonder we had problems in that war. Too many of our fellows let the war silence their consciences. They were hollow men.

My faith was on the line from the day I arrived in Vietnam. When Lt. Rambo found out I was a minister, he bought an electric guitar, a microphone, and an amplifier with navy money so I could hold religious services. I never saw a real chaplain, except for a guy who moved from base to base, whose only real job seemed to be to hand out tests for advancement in rank. So I became the unofficial chaplain of the base.

I never held regular services on Sunday morning. There wasn't even a designated schedule. When the Spirit presented the opportunity, I would get as many as possible together, pick the guitar, and teach them some gospel choruses. There was a little laughter from some, but I went right ahead. Then I would give a message. I would stand up right in the barracks and hold the microphone and preach. (Sometimes I went to the library if it was during the daytime and real hot, because the library was air-conditioned, quiet, and clean.) These services didn't occur that often; only a few times during the weeks we were in Sa Dec. My crewmates generally came—with a sort of snickering loyalty—and a few guys from other teams. Lt. Rambo came once. He really surprised me. He kidded me, but I could tell he respected me for being gutsy enough to say what I believed in.

I didn't always thunder at them from the Bible— sometimes we talked informally—but if I saw ten or fifteen guys there, I'd take the Bible in one hand, hold the microphone in the other, and go to town. I preached against sin to those boys. They would make fun of me in response, yet they stayed. And they hadn't come just to ridicule me. The truth about their lives made them uncomfortable; so, drawn and repulsed, they stayed and heckled. I got on them pretty good sometimes. I would say, "Guys, the day is going to come when your sin will come back to haunt you, to bite you like a snake." Then I would expound a biblical text about sin, repentance, forgiveness, and a changed life. They weren't great messages, but the guys felt the heat sometimes and at least had their consciences prodded.

Most of the guys lived with bad consciences, if they hadn't already become deaf to that still, small voice. A lot of them would come to me after a night in the bar or the brothel and say, "Roever, I know this isn't right." One guy had been brought up Pentecostal, a tall, lanky fellow. I wish

I had gotten to know him better, but he wasn't on the boats. He was part of the support crews who would take care of ammunition, arms, and supplies, and maintain the boats while in dock.

One evening, I was sitting out in a jeep—not going anywhere, just sitting there writing letters—when he came up and sat down beside me. He was drunk and he was crying and he said, "I'm so sorry. I know this isn't right. My momma raised me right. You do so good over here. How do you do it? How do you keep from doing the things we are doing? I know this isn't right." He kept going back to his momma. His conscience was killing him.

I knew there wasn't any sense talking to him. He was bombed and I knew that the next day, if he remembered what he had done, he would hate me for having listened to him. So I said, "I will pray with you, but there is not much going to change you until you want to be changed. There is nothing I can do. I'm here if you want to talk, but it's not going to do any good at the moment, considering the state you're in." That was shortly before I was transferred on to Tan An, and I never saw the guy again.

I did a lot of preaching against adultery. Some of those guys were married, and the access to infidelity was too convenient. The girls weren't even discreet. (There was no need to be discreet since prostitution wasn't illegal.) They were lined up on the street like tomatoes in a grocery store. They knew exactly how to attract the GIs—what provocative styles to wear and what gestures to use. In no time at all a guy would stumble half-blind with desire wherever the girl led him. Those girls were pros, yes indeed.

I watched these guys when they came back from the brothels. They always came back like they were in the pits, depressed and morose, but they'd brag about it later. Most of them, I'm sure, felt tremendously guilty. They were also afraid because they knew that every time they went to that brothel they were risking forms of venereal disease which had grown highly resistant to antibiotics.

The only time I ever got a glimpse of a brothel from the inside was when I was duped on my very first day at Sa Dec. I didn't know that "to get a haircut" was a euphemism for patronizing a prostitute. (This expression stemmed from the "barber shops" that often fronted for whorehouses.) This guy came up to me and said, "Man, you need a haircut. The CO will scalp you."

I hadn't had a haircut since training, so I thought the guy was sincere. I said, "Let's do it right now." So we walked out of the compound and headed into town.

He took me to this big white house with a little fence out in front, and we sat down in a kind of waiting room. I noticed right away that the smell wasn't the smell of hair tonics and shaving cream. It smelled like flowers and strong perfumes. I said, "Who cuts the hair?" He looked over and grinned at me just as a girl stepped out into the waiting room still buttoning up.

"Next," she said.

Then I knew where I was. I looked at him and I could have knocked his teeth out, but, instead, I said aloud, "Jesus, forgive me for being so naive." I felt as though I had sinned just being there. I walked out that door fast.

Incidentally, that guy was the very first person I led to the Lord in Vietnam. He was saved one day on patrol right on the boat. We were sitting up on the bow in a wide part of the river, totally safe out there. The guys were fooling around, swimming, drinking beer. This fellow and I got to talking, and he asked me about my faith: why I preached and why I sang gospel music. When I told him how I gave my heart to Jesus, the guy got tears in his eyes and I knew he was ready. I didn't think he had any religious training. I said, "If I help you, would you pray?"

He said, "Yeah." He looked around to see if the other guys were watching him, but they weren't paying any attention. They thought we were just up there shooting the breeze. I led him in a sinner's prayer. He was scheduled to go home in a week or so. He never opened up to me in any way about his life that showed why he made his decision, and I didn't ask questions. I just pray he kept his commitment.

So my faith was not something I kept hidden from the other men, and I took a lot of harassment as a result. Yet, I was human, too.

When we got orders to go from Sa Dec to Tan An, we were told we were relieving yet another company with a 90 percent casualty rate. Now that was the rumor; I can't vouch for its truth. Rumor or not, when I heard that, I thought, *This is it, this is where Vietnam hits me. It's going to kill me. I'll die here.* I became very depressed. I remember writing a letter to my brother. It began, "Dear Al, I wish I was home. I have a bad feeling about the world now." Then I went on to tell him that I felt like I was going to get hit. I can still remember every word of that letter. I tried to say it humorously, but I wanted him to know that I was frightened. I wanted to tell somebody of my fears.

Obviously, I was depressed because I thought I might die. What got to me about death more than anything else was the loss of Brenda. I just couldn't face the thought that I wouldn't be able to hold her again. I don't think I ever even thought about the physical suffering of dying. That's not what I was afraid of; I was afraid of not finishing my life with Brenda. To me death meant the loss of a future, the loss of *the* future with Brenda.

The night before transferring to Tan An, my depression got to me, and the guys could sense it. Those guys could smell my weakness like a shark smells blood, and they moved in for the kill. They didn't like my singing gospel songs; they didn't like my not going to the brothel; they didn't like my standing against their sin. They spotted their chance to break me, and they said to me, "Let's go get something cold to drink."

So we went over to the bar and I began playing some pool. Pervert Number Two said, "Let me buy. What do you want to drink?"

"Get me some grapefruit juice," I said.

Most of the guys used the grapefruit juice as a mixer with booze. One of the favorite drinks, a "salty dog," was grapefruit juice mixed with vodka. You can't really smell or taste the vodka, but you can feel it warm on your throat. Despite my request, I ended up with a salty dog. I knew something was peculiar right away because there was salt around the rim of the glass, and as soon as I put the drink to my mouth, I knew it was spiked.

But I didn't care because I thought, *This is it.* I feel now that all hell was saying at that moment, "We got him, boys," because I drank it right down. They told me the next day that I drank seventeen of them. I really don't know, but I know those guys put another in my hand as soon as the glass was empty. And I knew what I was doing. I can't say I didn't know.

Man, pretty soon I went to hit that cue ball and there were two of them. My stick went right between them. I mean, I missed the shot completely. Soon after, my head flapped down and I whacked my face on that slate table. I tried to stand up but couldn't. Finally I staggered to my feet. In only an hour-and-a-half or so I'd gotten smashed, dead drunk— for the only time in my life.

I have never liked the taste of alcohol, so I had a natural disinclination against drinking. But in this case I could hardly taste the alcohol, I couldn't smell it; there weren't the usual cues to put me off. It was so easy. With my drunkenness, however, came the feeling of betraying my Lord— just like Judas.

I staggered out of the bar and made my way, falling, staggering, falling again, and, in the end, crawling over to the showers. I crawled underneath the shower wall from the outside, reached up, and turned on the water, still with all my clothes on. I sat cross-legged on the floor of that shower, totally dazed and disoriented. I probably had enough alcohol in me to kill me—you can die of alcoholic poisoning.

I sat there with the water running and these guys came

through—most of them drunk too—laughing their freaking heads off. They absolutely, dearly loved it. The water was just pouring over me, keeping me conscious. I finally got up and started lurching, soaking wet, toward the barracks, and then I began throwing up. It just poured out of me—saving my life. Somehow I managed to crawl up into my bunk, at the top of a triple-tiered stack. I rolled right off that bunk— fell six feet and landed on the floor—but I was too numb to feel a thing. I crawled back up. I fell out a second time and whacked my head on the floor. The third time I managed to stay in the bunk. By then I was hurting. I lay in that bed with the whole building spinning in circles, clutching the mattress like it was a rodeo bull that had never been successfully ridden. When my stomach began to turn upside down I fell out of the bunk, but landed on my feet this time, and staggered out the door, where I started throwing up again. This went on until four o'clock in the morning, when I finally fell asleep.

Two hours later we were all awakened. We were transferring to Tan An that day. Needless to say, I had a hard time trying to get my head together. Out on the boat, we carried a five-gallon jug of ice water, and, I'm telling you, I drank every drop of water in that jug during the day-long trip, through small canals and big rivers. I've since learned that alcohol dehydrates you, but I didn't know then why I felt like I was dying from thirst. We traveled in an armada, the boats loaded down with all our gear, running at half-speed to conserve fuel so we wouldn't have to stop to refuel.

During the whole trip I don't think I said ten words to the guys. But they were watching me. My body was aching, but I was hurting spiritually worse than I was hurting physically. I apologized to them: "Guys, I'm sorry. I let you down. I let myself down. But you can bet your life I'll never get drunk again."

And I never did. That was sixteen years ago and just the thought of drinking booze still makes me nauseous.

The depression prompted by the move to Tan An lasted

only a day or two, but the remorse from having let down the Lord in my drunkenness lasted about a week. I couldn't stop brooding on my compromise. It was like seeing my mother's hurt eyes and knowing that I had done that to the Lord Jesus. I had blown it. In fact, the depression got so bad that the guys seemed to sense that I was all the more vulnerable and they stepped up their efforts to tempt me.

One morning I got so tired of the pressure that I said to myself, "I can't go on with this. I've had it. I'm going to do what they do and be like they are."

That very afternoon, we got a batch of mail and there was a letter for me from Rev. E. R. Anderson saying that by proxy the North Texas District Council of the Assemblies of God Church was granting me a license to preach. That broke the depression more than anything else. I had a card that said I was still very much in fellowship with those brethren back home. On the very day that I'm saying, *I'm giving up,* God was saying, *Hey, I'm promoting you. What are you giving up for?*

I felt like I had just been slapped in the face by a loving father. I can't help but believe He probably grinned and said, *You'll get over it. I don't like what you did, but I forgive you; now get on with your life. And remember, My grace is sufficient for you, because My grace is perfected in weakness.* God was taking the opportunity to show me my entire dependency on Christ, to let me see that I shouldn't trust in my own personal righteousness. I had to depend on the Lord. In this I started to leave behind an Old Testament faith, my models of Samson and the prophets, and began to look more directly to the Master of whom all the Old Testament heroes were but types, manifestations of the various aspects of His being. He, Christ alone, embodied the collective experience of those who had foreshadowed Him, and gathered it to a greatness of which the most righteous among them were hardly capable of dreaming.

The Lord certainly never let me question His grace. That

letter from Rev. Anderson was God's grace to me at the exact time when I needed it. God was saying, *Dave, I love you; that's behind you. You fell but I'll pick you up. Find your strength in Me, not in yourself.* But until that letter came, I was so disappointed in myself that I resisted hearing God's word of forgiveness.

10

*T*he Tan An compound was located west of Saigon. The Mekong River splits into two tributaries west of Saigon: the major branch is called the Vam Co, which itself splits into small tributaries called the Vam Co Tay and the Vam Co Dong. Sa Dec was on the Mekong and Tan An was on the Vam Co Tay. We were close to Cambodia the whole time, which accounts for the danger of our duties because the North Vietnamese infiltrated South Vietnam through Cambodia. At one point the north-south Cambodian border cuts way in toward Saigon in sort of a parrot's beak shape. The parrot's beak was extremely dangerous territory because the enemy could pile up men and supplies in neutral territory that was within striking distance of Saigon. American troops weren't yet permitted into Cambodia, so the mission of the navy's riverboat patrols was to shut down the VC movement of arms, ammunition, and personnel from Cambodia into the area around Saigon.

When the bombing of the Ho Chi Minh Trail was stopped, the enemy flooded down that trail through Laos and Cambodia directly into that parrot's beak. We had proof that the bombing of the Ho Chi Minh Trail was effective, because when it stopped, the North Vietnamese Army poured through. All we had was a few little fiberglass boats against the brunt of the North Vietnamese forces. At home everybody saw the Americans as big strong men fighting puny little Vietcong teenagers. But we were up against a major force. After they separated from the Vam Co, the Vam Co Dong and Vam Co Tay curved around in opposite directions. Our division's job was to patrol the Vam Co Tay up to the Cambodian border.

Tan An was a small village of about three thousand people, with a big army base across town from our compound which was right on the river. In fact, our barracks was a floating barge, called a mobile base two (MB2). An MB2 was a big flat barge with a superstructure on top, built like ship's quarters with hatches between rooms, which were air-conditioned, extremely modern, well-lighted, and hospital-clean. About one hundred guys were quartered in an MB2, in bunks stacked three high but laid out at different heights so you couldn't just look from one side of the barracks to the other. Under each bunk mattress there was a storage compartment about six inches deep the width and length of the entire bed. Additional locker units stood nearby.

Our boats were tied up right alongside the barge, which itself was not all that secure. Because there were no guards or defenses up or downstream, we posted a guard all the time who was to be on the lookout for anything floating down the river. We worried about water mines, and when the guards saw something they weren't sure of, they would set off concussion grenades. That meant that every now and then we would be startled by a loud explosion in the water.

Every aspect of life was more tense and stressful at Tan An than at Sa Dec. We had no regular daily schedule, but would go out on long patrols, often several nights running. Enemy action picked up. Our relations with one another got more tense, too, with the guys getting on each other's nerves and cussing one another out.

I had no opportunity to hold services at Tan An. For one thing, the guitar and microphone had to stay at Sa Dec. I did have an old Stella guitar and I would sit around and pick that guitar and sing for my own enjoyment and edification, but I was never able to get a group of guys together. I couldn't even get into a daily schedule of private devotions because there was no routine that permitted anything to be done on a regular basis. You had to be ready at any time to go into action. Sometimes I would pray at my bunk, but I would almost always be harassed. If I read my Bible I was asking for trouble. Some guy would come along and try to flip it shut, then walk on by, usually saying something like "You _____ preacher." I finally decided that maintaining peace with my teammates was more important than making a big deal out of my devotional life.

I got the nickname "Preacher Man" after moving to Tan An. When our bunk assignments were made I ended up with a couple of guys close by who were a pain. The guy who bunked right above me became my chief antagonist. He and two other guys came up with my nicknames, "Preacher Man," "Dudley Do-right," and "Doctor Dolittle." I gave them nicknames of my own: "Pervert Number One," "Pervert Number Two," and "Pervert Number Three." These nicknames, on both sides, weren't truly malicious; they could be used in a friendly or stinging way depending on the context. Pervert Number One was a big stocky fellow with dark hair, a roundish face, and a captivating smile, on the rare occasions when he smiled. He was a smart, crafty guy who had a gift for being outright mean. With one tongue lashing he could make you feel like the loneliest nerd on God's earth. He could motivate the other guys to reinforce this opinion by their actions. A natural leader, he could make anyone an outcast.

I kept civilian clothes over there, some nice shoes and sport shirts and dress slacks, and I wore them when I wasn't on patrol. I was the only guy there who would put on decent clothes when he wanted to relax. The guys would really mock me because they knew intuitively that caring about my appearance helped keep my moral guard up. Dressing like that reminded me that God has conferred on man a dignity greatly superior to his other earthly creations. Pervert Number One, smart as he was, saw through to the meaning of these manners and was especially antagonized by them.

There would be times when my teammates were getting ready to go out and have a night on the town and they would say something like, "Come on, Preacher Man. You come with us."

Sometimes they would bring one or two girls right into the barracks and pass her around. (This was strictly forbidden, of course, but they did it anyway.) I just walked out. Keeping away from these scenes was the only thing I could do. I escaped to a quiet corner of the barracks to dwell on memories of Brenda and listen to cassette tapes of her voice—the sound of which always renewed my spirit and strengthened my conscience.

Then there were the pornographic movies they brought in. I was more frightened of them than of the girls; it was easier to stick around to watch them. But I knew that I didn't want to fill my mind with that rot. Some of these movies were made right there in Tan An; guys would come back bragging about their starring roles.

Alcohol and sex abounded, but I never saw any drugs among the guys around me. The evidence is clear that a lot of GIs used heroin, hashish, and pot in Vietnam. I'm sure the main reason why none of our guys got into drugs was because we were doing such dangerous work in small, closely knit teams. If anybody had been high, we couldn't have trusted him. He would have put the rest of us in danger of being killed. It was almost an unwritten rule: anybody using dope would be eliminated by his own comrades. Too much was at stake.

During my time at Tan An, enemy activity increased steadily. We ran into more frequent sniper fire, more ambushes, large and small. Sa Dec was R and R compared to Tan An. As I've indicated, we were on twenty-four-hour

call without regular shifts. We had perhaps ten hours to
relax between shifts, which could run as long as sixteen or
eighteen hours. Still the commanding officers tried not to
work us until sheer fatigue produced lackadaisical atti-
tudes that could prove deadly. It was essential to remain
alert.

We did our job well. We shut down those rivers to the
communists. They ambushed us to scare us off, but it didn't
work. We kept coming back, and they never gained control
of the rivers. They had the manpower, but we had superior
firepower and superior equipment to move that firepower
around. All they had were battered old sanpans and they
could attack us only by employing hit-and-run tactics. The
best thing they could do was ambush us.

Our patrols were largely sent out in response to intelli-
gence information about enemy activity. Our reconnaissance planes took infrared photographs at night and used a
form of radar that was sensitive to temperatures. It could
pick up the collective body heat of enemy troops. Helicopters were always reporting information about enemy
activity and little Pipercub spotter planes also checked out
enemy movement. We generally had fairly reliable information on enemy movements, so we knew when and where to
go. Actually, our best source of information was often the
chou Hois—the surrendering VC—who would spill their
guts. They would often tell us what was about to happen
instead of sticking to what had already happened: the latter
being the strategy of true patriots.

Once, for instance, aerial photography had spotted what
appeared to be Vietcong R and R camps just over the Cambodian border. I volunteered to go with the sniper and Lt.
Rambo on a special assignment to check them out. The
three of us took a small fiberglass boat powered by two
small but strong Johnson outboard motors. I carried an
M-60 (the same gun that Stallone's Rambo uses in the
movie), the sniper carried his .30-caliber game-hunting
rifle, and Lt. Rambo carried the most unusual weapon I

ever saw in Vietnam, a fully automatic, sawed-off 12–gauge shotgun: one bad weapon.

We made our way cautiously up some shallow little man-made canals, certainly across the border into Cambodia. As we rounded a curve in a tiny canal, we surprised fifty to a hundred stark-naked Vietcong all bathing in the canal. There was indeed a large R and R center up in there. All of the enemy's weapons were stacked in a big pile in the clearing up on the bank. All of their shoes were lined up down along the river. All their clothes were piled together, and they had a stack of little bamboo cages in which they had caught snakes to eat. When they looked up and saw us coming, the look on their faces was indescribable. We were as surprised as they were, and I know that each of us was in a quandary about what to do. Having crossed the Cambodian border, we didn't want an international incident, so I started firing right above their heads. Those guys scattered in every direction. They took off naked as jay-birds into the jungle. One guy even swam the canal and took off on the other side. None of them went near the weapons. They knew if they went near their weapons my aim would suddenly improve. They must have praised Buddha that we didn't kill them all. This all happened in a matter of seconds.

We were there to search out the area and to find out how much of what was coming in from where by whom. And we sure found out. The enemy ran off, leaving all of their weapons, their clothing, their supplies, even their shoes.

We beached the boat and checked out the camp. In empty mortar cans we found huge supplies of carbide which they used to give light at night. We burned all their clothes and their shoes; we destroyed their food and released the snakes. We burned the weapons with a plastic explosive called C4. We destroyed everything. That incident ended up being more comical than anything else, although it was scary enough heading back through those little canals. This happened about three weeks before I was injured.

Our job, as I said, was to patrol the Vam Co Tay. One section of the river made a kind of S-curve, although the bottom half had been cut by a canal to eliminate one of the loops. For some reason, that S-curve was an area where there was an unusual amount of communist activity. For a long time nobody seemed to be able to get a handle on what the VC were doing there. We had to flush out that canal. Nobody wanted to go through it. It was narrow and shallow and the boat would occasionally scrape bottom. One night, because of the poor navigation of a substitute coxswain, we even ran aground at low tide and were stuck high and dry, sitting ducks, for twelve hours until the tide came back in.

Another day when we were patrolling that canal I had a strong sense of the enemy's presence. All the signs were there. You could see where they would beach; you could see where they would cross the canal, yet there was no visible evidence besides the likelihood of the spot itself. Everything was as quiet as could be. More out of boredom than anything else, I decided to clean the guns, test them, shoot them. So I called in on the radio to get clearance. (You had to get permission from headquarters to fire if you weren't being fired upon. When there were friendly villages nearby, you had to get clearance to return fire *even if you were being fired upon.*)

Permission was granted for us to H and I—"harass and intimidate." To line up my sights, I decided to take aim at a big old white tomb with a cross on it (left over, like many Christian objects and buildings, from the French colonial period) about five hundred yards away in a field. I figured I would take a pot shot with one of my front 50–caliber guns and see where the tracer would go. I put in tracers and squeezed off one round. Bam. I must have missed it a hundred yards to the right. I pulled the front of the gun over toward the other gun and tried again. I missed again, but I was closer. I shot several more times. Finally I gave up adjusting the aim of single shots. I decided to walk it on target, like you do in a fire-fight. So I connected the second gun, pushed the button on the electronic firing mechanism, and starting pumping away. I walked it right on in. I was low when I started firing but in a second or two I had it on the tomb. You could see tracers ricocheting and concrete dust flying everywhere. Eventually I aimed for the cross and blew it right off, the whole top of the tomb sliding right off behind it.

We didn't know it, but there was an army spotter in a Pipercub right above us, and we were scaring this dude to death. We were firing away and he didn't know what was going on. He was trying to get us on our radio, but the army spotters weren't on the same frequency as the navy boats, so it took him awhile. Finally he picked us up and started screaming, "Stop firing, stop firing. What's wrong? You got a fire-fight? Where's the enemy? We'll help you."

I felt like a jerk, but I hadn't known he was up there. He should have let us know. I said, "I'm sorry, man, we had no idea you were up there. No one told us." I told him we had clearance and that I was just doing some H and I out here.

"What are you hitting?" he asked.

I mentioned the old tomb and told him where it was so he could check it out. He flew over the tomb site and a couple seconds later he comes on the radio yelling his head off. "You won't believe what I'm seeing. That's no tomb; that's an arsenal—full of guns and ammunition."

He called in a big back-up team, and we stayed on location because we figured the enemy knew what we had done. The army flew a team in right away to check it out and found an incredible cache of supplies and equipment. I got a medal from the Vietnamese army for discovery of an enemy cache—purely by accident.

We learned something important about the enemy that day: They were making use of our respect for the dead. We weren't graverobbers, and they knew we usually respected burial sites. (Looking back on that incident, I'm aware of how callous my actions were, whatever their fortuitous results.) We discovered they were using a number of tombs in that area to sleep in or to hide in during the day before moving on at night. We found out they had even fabricated fake cardboard tombs which they would fold up and carry around with them at night. Then during the day they would set them up and sleep in them. They were always far enough away so that their tombs looked real to us, but there they were, snoozing away almost under our noses.

Another day we went through that canal and the VC suddenly opened fire in an ambush. Then the craziest thing happened. We heard a loud explosion from the bank and the firing stopped. Soon a group of ARVN soldiers appeared on the bank laughing and shouting. There had been an ARVN operation going on there that nobody had told us about. We didn't know they were there, but they were coming up to ambush the VC from behind. One of the ARVNs told us, "We were coming up behind the VC but we couldn't open fire on them or we would have hit you. But you didn't see us and when you opened fire on the VC from the boats, you almost killed us."

Obviously that's not what they found funny. The reason they were laughing and shouting was because of what happened to the VC ambush. Apparently an old VC fellow had a B-40 rocket on his shoulder and was aiming dead on our front boat: my boat. I was driving the boat that day, and, bored, I threw the throttles wide open in order to blow mud and water out of the boat engine pumps. Anyway, I hit those throttles and the boat leapt forward just as the old man was preparing to fire. To keep his aim on the boat he turned, and when he squeezed the trigger, he hit an old tree stump not six inches in front of him. The rocket never even got out of the tube. It just hit the stump, and, wham, it blew up and killed him and everybody around him.

The ARVNs were already mutilating the man's body. Both the Vietcong and the ARVN forces would usually follow the same conqueror's ritual. It was sick, and it was gross. But that's what they did. They would disembowel him, too. We heard stories about one of our U.S. boats where the crew fell asleep and drifted into the bank. The Vietcong killed them, decapitated them, and left them on display. But I never saw stuff like that. I heard about a lot of atrocities that I can neither confirm nor deny. And since these stories helped keep us alert, our officers didn't do much to stop them.

Let me say that our team and most of our forces treated the people we captured with absolute decency. The ARVN forces conducted themselves differently. At times I questioned whether we were compromising the goal of America in South Vietnam by tolerating the behavior of the South Vietnamese army, and sometimes that of our own undisciplined military personnel. I wondered occasionally if the South Vietnamese would be able to make a democratic form of government work even if they had the chance. But, to be honest, in the midst of surviving from day to day and doing my job, I didn't think much about these larger political questions. I just hoped that if these people could ever be free long enough, they would work out their problems. I hoped that a basic sense of morality would evolve. Yet in my heart, I couldn't imagine how that could happen without the values of the Christian faith. That's why in 1974 and 1975 I went back to Vietnam as a missionary evangelist. I wanted to see Truth come to Vietnam, not democracy at that juncture, but just plain righteousness. I figure if you get the gospel preached in any country, it has a way of straightening the place out.

I don't see how democracy can flourish when greed and evil grow unchecked. Democracy calls for forms of self-restraint which a pagan culture just doesn't exhibit or require. That's of course why our job in South Vietnam was so difficult, if not impossible.

Add to these difficulties the tragedy at home in America where—instead of praying for us—many people were marching to exhibit that their sympathies lay with the Vietcong. This had a devastating effect on morale.

Americans at home were too often the gullible victims of

what I know from firsthand experience to be Vietcong propaganda. You can believe the Vietcong tried their best to create situations in which Americans appeared blameworthy for destroying the country they were claiming to save. Typically, for example, the VC would set up their ambushes at sites between the Americans and a vulnerable open village. Their plan was to open fire on us and hope that we would lack restraint and start firing back indiscriminately, killing many more civilians than enemy troops. Then they'd get pictures of it, put it in newspapers, write letters, and tell the world what bad boys we were. That was the major strategy we had to guard against. We had to know at all times where we were and where the villages were.

The Vietcong knew that the indiscriminate killing of innocent people along with the enemy was totally unacceptable to Americans. I agree. I would rather the enemy go unpunished than the innocent be destroyed. I can tell you that the teams I was associated with did their best to protect the civilians.

The Vietcong fought, and finally won, the war using such tactics. Because they knew that we would not do anything likely to destroy innocent people, they lived among the civilians. They used the babies; they used the mothers and the wives; they used the women and the old people to hide behind. The communists literally hid behind the women's skirts to win that war. (These are the basic tactics of terrorist warfare; the same tactics the PLO have employed successfully for so long in Lebanon.)

An incident involving a civilian caught in the middle still sticks in my mind. We were ambushed. We opened fire, and in the skirmish, a little boy and the big water buffalo he was riding were killed. We don't know if it was our bullets or the communists' that hit the boy. (I'll tell you one thing, you can bet your life there were times when the communists turned their guns on civilians to make it look like we had committed atrocities.) Anyway, an old man came running at us swinging a hoe in rage. He was screaming and cursing—I couldn't make out what he was saying—but the white mouse told me, "He's mad at you because you killed his water buffalo." The old man said nothing about the kid.

The kids, oh yes, the kids. What that war did to the children pained me most.

Not long before my injury, I was given command of the boat now and again. I was being trained as the next captain, taking over from Bob, my third captain whose stint was almost up. I became curious about a little man-made canal off the main river that we had never checked out, which, indeed, wasn't even on the map. We had learned there was a small village up that canal, so I suggested we do a little exploring. We hadn't been under enemy pressure for several days, so the two boats in our team took off up this canal. It was so shallow that we were scraping bottom; if the tide had been going out, we would have been in big trouble. Fortunately, the tide was coming in, and navigation became easier as we went along. The canal ended in a sort of *cul de sac* at the village of Tu Tua, which seemed to have escaped the war. The canal was narrow so I made sure we maneuvered the boats around for a quick getaway if necessary. Then I bumped my boat up on the bank and leaped off the front onto the rickety little pier.

I walked up through the village. Children were everywhere—so many of them that I wondered if Tu Tua was an oasis in the midst of the desert of war, a place where people brought their children to keep them safe. True or not, there were an inordinate number of women and children in the village, and very few men, all of whom were old.

I walked by a little casket company where an old fellow sat out front engraving Buddhist coffins. We also saw a warehouse, in which they kept big blocks of ice, hauled in from Saigon, completely insulated with rice hulls.

But the kids wouldn't come near me. They stayed back just beyond the reach of my gun butt and looked as if they were afraid I would hit them. I was surprised by their obvious fear, because I figured they must have been some of the same kids who had fearlessly accosted us down on the river, and with whom I had begun to make friends. When our boats would come by, these little kids would paddle out in their tiny sanpans, hold out their hands, and say, *"Chop, chop,* GI, you give me *chop, chop."* They wanted food. I loved seeing the children, but I was always nervous with them around the boat because of the potential for mishap.

I remember one day when this kid kept coming back even after I told him to beat it. He was all alone in his little boat, and he sat right up in the bow. *"Chop chop,* you give me *chop chop."* He was persistent. Finally I couldn't ignore him. He was a cute little guy, I said, *"la day,"* come alongside, kid. I reached down to help pull him up in the boat, but he must have thought I was going to hit him—these kids were skittish, man, and I couldn't blame them. When he leaned back, he fell off the padded rag he was sitting on. That's when I noticed he didn't have any legs. The kid had no legs. I thought he had been sitting cross-legged. In Vietnamese, I asked him what had happened. He told me he had stepped on a "booby trap"—he said that word in English. I pulled the kid up in the boat and held him in my lap. I was fighting the tears, let me tell you. It's one thing to see the enemy dead, or even civilians; the dead don't hurt. It's another thing to see people suffering, especially innocent children.

I held this poor child up against me and started scrounging around for some food. I found one of the cornflake candy bars included in the combat rationing package. We never ate them. We just threw them in the bilge under the engine cover. The cellophane wrapper was all greasy, but the inside was clean, so I opened it up and gave it to the kid. You could see he was in heaven eating that old candy bar. While he was eating, I noticed that his thumb had been smashed. (He told me that he had learned to walk on his hands, and that someone had stepped on his thumb.) I could see that his thumbnail had actually separated and was hanging on by a "thread" of connective tissue. It must have caused a lot of pain or he would have pulled it off. You could see the bloody pus oozing out from under the cuticle and running down his arm as he ate. The kid was going to get gangrene for sure, and I thought, *Lord, he's lost his legs and now he's going to lose his arm, maybe his life.*

I sat him up on the engine cover, propped him against the gunwale, and started rummaging through the first-aid kit while he ate his candy bar. I washed his hands and then poured Mercurochrome all over his thumb. By then, the kid had trust in me. I jerked off that loose thumbnail, like you might pull out a child's baby tooth, and he—despite the pain—just kept eating. Then I began squeezing out the bloody pus, about gagging myself and still fighting off tears. He would look at me and then he would eat and then he would look at me and sometimes he would wince a little from the pain. But the more I squeezed, the more stuff came out until I felt like I'd have to squeeze his whole arm out to get that wound clean. So I made a note of our coordinates and eventually called in a medical operations team to go in there and give that kid some attention. I got the little fellow's thumb cleaned up as best I could and then covered it with a huge gauze bandage. I ended up taping his whole hand to keep it clean. He started waving his hand at the kids on the bank. They were all envious because he had received something, and they hadn't. I set him back in his boat, said good-bye, and he paddled away.

I met up with that kid not long afterward in more pleasant circumstances brought about by my own foolishness. Out on the boat one day, I was bored and decided to detonate a satchel charge underwater. I tossed that thing overboard, but when the charge didn't sink, I got scared. It must have been only about five inches below the surface when it detonated—instead of the twenty feet I had anticipated. When the charge exploded, it lifted the back of the boat right out of the water and spun us completely around. I almost "blew us out of the water." We got to laughing and screaming. Then a miracle happened—I call it a miracle because it reminds me of one of Jesus' own miracles. The charge must have landed on top of a school of fish because thousands, I mean thousands, of fish immediately floated to the surface, belly up, some of them dead but a lot just knocked unconscious. The children on the bank of the river saw what had happened. They piled into their little boats, and I mean an entire flotilla of children came roaring out there and started scooping up fish by the hundreds. They were loading their boats down until I thought they would sink. That same boy with no legs was among them, and he was shouting, "GI, you number one, GI, you number one." He loved me.

It was only a couple of days after I blew up the fish for everyone that we went up the canal to Tu Tua, and I assume that some of the same kids lived in that village. That's why I was surprised that they were so skittish. Of course, I had caught all these people off guard. They weren't expecting anybody up in there, much less two boats. When I saw their fear, I went back to my boat and took off every weapon I carried, my pistol, my K-bar knife. I even took off my ammunition belt. And when I returned to the village, those kids came up real close.

One kid, only about five or six years old, walked up to me and touched my hand, then jumped back to see if I was going to hit him. He came back a second time and touched me, then jumped back out of the way again. The third time I saw him coming, I said to myself, *I'm going to have fun with this little turkey.* When he reached out to touch my hand, I grabbed his. His eyes rolled up in their sockets and he let out such a wail of terror you would have thought I was going to skin him alive. I gathered him up, pulled him in real tight, and held his little tummy up against my chest, trying to get him to quit kicking and screaming. He'd look up at me, then he'd scream some more, then he'd look up, then he'd scream some more. But gradually the screaming subsided, and I could feel his body relax, and finally he looked up at me and said, "GI, you number one."

When that little fellow relaxed, all the other kids just stormed me. They crawled up my legs, hung onto my arms, clamored up my back. One of them tried to climb from my shoulders up onto the perch of my head. I tried to waddle along with them on me and finally just collapsed under their weight. They were laughing. I was laughing. It felt so good to be making some child laugh instead of making a widow cry over her dead husband and her orphaned babies. The kids started chanting, *"Mop det, mop det, mop det."* I continued to play with them, wrestling with them on the ground. The sound of those children's happy voices came to me as the breath of God, scraping away my own callousness with the sandpaper of love. I wanted to cry. The only softening tears are those that come from joy, not anger. The tears I'd shed over causing pain had only hardened me, like water when added to the heavy powder of concrete.

When I got ready to leave, the kids said, "You okay, GI, you number one *mop det*, you come back, you come back tomorrow." They could speak a little broken English; most people in Vietnam could. It troubled me that they could speak broken English, and yet they acted as though we were the first Americans they'd ever seen.

As dirty as a pig from rolling in the dirt, I went back to the boat and told the guys, "We're coming back here tomorrow."

They said, "No way. They'll kill us, man, they'll set an ambush."

I said, "How do the VC know we are coming back tomorrow? I didn't tell them we were. I just told the kids."

The fellows said, "That's all it takes."

"We're taking our chances. We're coming back. We can do more to win this war by making friends than by killing enemies."

The next day we went back. It was my command decision. As we turned up the little canal, we spotted a kid waiting there—the same guy I had held in my arms—

almost as though he had been appointed to keep watch. Our boats were unmarked, so he really looked everybody over. I was standing up on the bow like Captain Cook. When we started up the canal, the kid took off running as fast as he could, screaming at the top of his lungs. We could hear him running through the village shouting *"Mop det, mop det, mop det,"* and soon all the kids started coming out into the clearing. They about swamped the boat at the dock. I stepped off, again without weapons of any kind, and walked into the village. I swear I emptied that village of every kid. Mothers stepped out of huts and watched in obvious amazement as the kids flocked to me. I felt like the Pied Piper of Tu Tua.

I played with the children again that day. I didn't have any treats with me, but when we came back on the third day, I took a box of popcorn. I had recently received a package from Brenda with a big plastic bag of popcorn stuffed around the contents. When I arrived with that box of popcorn, a sea of kids jumped up and down chanting *"Mop det, mop det."* It was a little bit of heaven. They mobbed me again and went wild over the food. The mothers loved it. They loved to see their children love me. That was the day I found out what *mop det* meant: Fatso!

I knew that we would have to quit soon, that the VC would soon enough find out and take advantage of our lowered guard to ambush us. But the fourth day we went back in there.

As we neared the canal, I saw smoke drifting up over the trees coming from the direction of the village. When we got to the mouth of the canal we saw the Vietcong had moved in there and were punishing the place: burning the rice fields, burning the hooches, asserting their authority by taking over a village of women and children. My heart pounded with fear. I just prayed the children were safe. The U.S. military had already detected the Vietcong raid, because, as we were getting ready to head up the canal, American helicopters began flying over and we saw American tanks coming down through the bush. We could also hear machine gun fire from the area of the village itself—fire that could only have come from communist troops since there weren't any Americans in there yet.

The communists tried to get out, but they weren't quick enough. Our tanks caught them, and I watched that village being totally wiped out. I watched the army tanks pull up on top of big bunkers full of VC and crush them. Our boys went in like gangbusters. When the tanks had done their job, we went in behind them to check out the village. We saw the dead children—gunned down not by tank shells or helicopter artillery but by Vietcong machine guns. When they knew the American troops were coming in, the VC had turned around and slaughtered the women and children, trying to make it look as if the Americans were responsible. They had killed all those little kids who had been crawling all over me and eating popcorn the day before.

You know what that does to your soul? Think about it, long and hard. I have.

We turned the boats around and came back out. From the boat, my team could still follow the movement of what was left of the enemy, so I got on the radio, ordered an air strike, called in the coordinates, and watched a jet—at my own command—drop bomb after bomb on what was left of Tu Tua. When the bombs detonated, we felt the reverberations from the explosions and saw the concussion rings spread out. I felt like I'd been slugged in the stomach.

This completed the terrible irony of the incident. Trying to be friendly, I had placed those women and children in jeopardy. The action of our army, in warding off the children's attackers, had turned those attackers into executioners. And I, the Pied Piper of Tu Tua, had finally been responsible for cremating the corpses of those children, of immolating the last vestiges of that village's existence. By my order, Tu Tua was blasted off the face of God's earth. I didn't speak as we headed back to the base. And I didn't cry. I had no tears, or if they were there, they set and dried in the concrete of my soul before they had a chance to fall.

After Tu Tua, I had it in me to volunteer to drop the bomb on Hanoi. I could understand what could make Colonel Kurtz in the movie *Apocalypse Now* scrawl across his journal, "Drop the bomb," or Joseph Conrad's Kurtz write, "Exterminate all the brutes."

Feelings like that were also, I think, largely the result of not knowing who the enemy was. He's a woman; he's a child; he's a face that smiles at you in the morning and tosses a grenade at you in the night. He cuts your hair in the morning and cuts your throat at night. She washes your clothes one day and strips them from your dead body the next. We felt that kind of frustration, that kind of confusion about who the enemy was. It would have been so nice if they would have worn a uniform instead of black "pajamas." Everybody wore black "pajamas."

What happened on a heart-crushing scale at Tu Tua happened in a thousand small ways every day. You try to act out of principle, with good motives. But even the good that you do, the good relations you build with the people, can become occasions for evil, like at Tu Tua. In such a situation, how do you maintain your principles? In the confusion, you tend to lose your moral and spiritual equilibrium and sound judgment. Your desire to differentiate the good guys from the bad guys grows weaker. Everyone not in the uniform of your country looks like the enemy.

That's why so many fellows came back and couldn't cope any more. All war is hell. But Vietnam was a faith-destroying, soul-shredding war, not only because of the erosion of moral principle on the battlefield and in the brothel, but because there was no confirmation upon our return that we had been fighting for worthwhile principles.

You could even say that the Vietcong terrorist tactics simulated on Whidbey Island were successfully practiced on us by our own people. What I mean is this: The Vietnam vet

Aboard a PBR in Vietnam, Dave sits on the gun tub of his .50 caliber machine gun. It was in this gun tub that Dave was later injured.

Above: Dave in the barracks at Mare Island near San Francisco.

Below: Training boats at Mare Island.

Dave on patrol in
Vietnam.

Below: Dave stands on
the bow of a PBR in
Sa Dec, holding the M-2
carbine he modified for
close order combat.

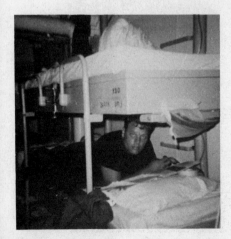

Dave on his bunk in
Mobil Base 2 at Tan An.

Above: Wearing his special services black beret, Dave stands in front of the twin gun mounts he designed and made while at Sa Dec.

Below: PBR in high speed pursuit.

came home to a people who, in fact, had accepted the materialistic assumptions of our Marxist enemy, not the *ideology* of communism but the *philosophic world* of communism. We came home to a people who had largely accepted that man *is* nothing more than a complicated animal.

Perhaps that is really why the Vietnam vet was shunned for so long. It wasn't only that we had lost the war, but that we had been asked to fight for ideals in which America no longer believed—the dignity of man, for example. Our very presence pronounced judgment against the hedonism which reigned in America when we returned. And so, many vets came back to a country that seemed one big POW camp, where your "needs" would be met if you were willing to "cooperate," to admit the stupidity of the war you had been fighting, to make your sense of self that of a hedonistic consumer, an animal in civilized garb. The country we left, the civilization we represented, was hardly to be found when we returned. The phrase frequently used to describe it all was, "Home is hell."

The war took a spiritual toll on me, too. But my moral principles were not dependent on confirmation by other people. They were founded on the Word of God. I kept one foot on the Rock, even if the other foot often slipped in the Mekong mud. I know that God hasn't forgotten those children of Tu Tua and that He will justly hold *all* accountable for their actions—including Dave Roever.

11

*A*n air of bitterness lingered heavily for several days after the incident at Tu Tua. Reports of enemy movement seemed to pick up dramatically. In July 1969, after the Tet Offensive, the enemy made considerable advances. I've heard from the communists themselves that they really felt as if they had lost the war in 1968.

I remember watching a BBC documentary while I was in England in which a North Vietnamese general said, "We lost the war in 1968 to the Americans. The Tet Offensive crushed us. But when we saw the antiwar demonstrations in America and the American youth in rebellion, we took new heart and began to fight again. The whole war turned in our favor."

From that point on, enemy activity in our area, through July of 1969, increased at an alarming rate. Saigon became the main objective, and since the parrot's beak was so close to Saigon, it became the front line. In that context, the little canal cutting through the lower section of the S-curve in the Vam Co Tay River became something of a concern to us again. We located a key crossing point in the S, right near the Cambodian border, and took on a fire-fight there one afternoon.

It was about six o'clock and the sun was already pretty low in the sky. The "magic hour" of dusk can lull you into a false sense of security, and I felt very much at ease that evening. I pulled out my beat-up old Stella guitar, which I often brought with me on the boat just to help pass the time. We were too close to the riverbanks, the river was entirely too narrow, for me to feel as secure as I did— picking that old guitar. I was thinking of Brenda and strumming some melancholy chords. I remember the incredible stillness and beauty of the evening as I sat there with my feet propped up on my guns. There wasn't even a hint of a breeze.

Then, as startling as someone slapping me in the face, a swish went right over the top of my head. My heart stopped. I could tell it was a B–40 rocket, fired from the bank of the river, obviously aimed at my head. The forward gunner was usually the first object of the enemy's attack. If they could knock him out, they eliminated two very powerful guns. But they missed from about forty yards. Right over my head. I was a big, still target—easy pickings. There was no way he should have missed me; he should at least have hit the boat. A B–40 is an antitank rocket containing two separate explosive charges. The first is designed to pierce armor plating. But if you want to knock out a tank, you have to do more than make a hole in it. So a second projectile inside the first explodes after the shell has penetrated the object of attack. Actually, the B–40 is often ineffective against a fiberglass boat because it can penetrate the fiberglass—and come out the other side of the hull without detonating. But he missed. I have never been able to recall what happened to my Stella guitar. Perhaps in my panic I tossed it out of my way, overboard. I never saw it again. I slid down from my perch on the guttering along the gunwale into the gun tub.

Small-arms fire began seconds after the initial rocket. All of us agreed later that thirteen rockets were fired. You might wonder how we kept track during a fire-fight. Almost subconsciously, instinctively, we'd learned to count to get an idea of the size of the attack, to determine how spread out the attack was, and to figure out how many guys were firing rockets. These rockets were probably coming from two guys. They were fired too quickly to come from one gun. They were certainly too close for comfort, but once we got moving we had a chance.

We got out and started making our firing runs. I shudder thinking of the times we turned that boat around and came back into the attack. It would have been so much easier to keep going, but our job was to keep heading back. We were the ducks on the belt: Let them shoot at you and see if they can hit you. The cover boat was going through it, too. They took seven rounds, making a total of twenty B–40s fired at us. I could feel the whack on the boat whenever a shell hit.

I took some shrapnel in the face that caught me right along my lower left eyelid. It was a tiny piece of metal that embedded itself down in there and hurt like fire. But I didn't feel anything wet: I wasn't bleeding, which meant that I was okay, if scared half to death. We continued making run after run until the enemy finally stopped.

Every time I blinked, it felt like something was slicing my eye. I couldn't get it out, and it was driving me buggy. As small as that piece of shrapnel was, I had to have some medical attention to remove it. So we called in a dust-off helicopter to lift me out. The captain was going to take the boat back to the compound to pick up more ammunition, and I would rejoin the team back at Tan An.

An army helicopter lifted me to a MASH type unit at the army post on the other side of Tan An. The doctor found a tiny piece of metal down in the membrane below the eyeball and picked it out. They wanted to put a patch over it, but I can't stand the feeling of trying to see out of only one eye, so I talked them out of the patch. They did put something in it to stop infection. Happily, the injury was minor and there were no complications.

When I was about to leave, I asked if I could get some transportation back to my compound so I wouldn't have to

walk the whole way through town. Not that I was lazy, but I
was anxious to rejoin the team—the flow of adrenalin during the attack had left me with the shakes. I was also just
plain nervous from the scare with my eye. But they told me
to walk. One guy, I remember, said, "Our motto around
here is: Dogs and sailors keep off the grass; dogs and sailors
walk."

I was a bit miffed, and, by dumb luck, I found a jeep out
front with the keys left in it. On a lark, I took off and drove
it all the way to our compound, but parked about a hundred
yards up river so that the evidence wouldn't be too obvious.

Then a bizarre thing happened. As I was walking down
the gangplank to the barge, Lt. Rambo stepped out of the
command communication center, about thirty feet to my
left. It was about ten o'clock. I started to greet him, but
didn't. He looked up, saw me under the light on the gangplank, and stared at me a second as if he were shocked. He
said, "Roever, what are you doing here?"

The thought flashed through my mind that he must have
thought that my patrol had never gone out, that we'd been
in town screwing around. (It had been known to happen.)
The punishment for playing hooky from patrol was severe.
So I felt compelled to defend myself. I said, "Lieutenant,
I've just come in on a dust-off. I got some shrapnel in my
eye, Sir, and they were fixing my eye over there at the army
medical unit. I just signed papers over at the army base for
their records."

The guy was obviously stunned. He said, "Roever, I know
that; I just talked to you on the radio an hour ago, and you
guys were under attack."

"Yes, Sir," I said. (We had made one radio communication
during the fire-fight, calling in a light duty fire team, which
means you get two or three helicopters for aerial support.)

"I heard that fire-fight on the radio," said Rambo, "and
when the dust-off was called in, I specifically heard that
the side of your face was blown off, the trunk of your body
had third-degree burns, and that your hands suffered blast

damage. I heard that over the radio." He still looked at me in disbelief, as if I were a ghost.

I, of course, was stunned, too. I said, "No Sir, no Sir, I'm fine. I just got some shrapnel in my eye. Nothing like that happened. Everybody is fine. None of the team got hurt."

So he came on over to the gangplank, we shook hands, and I went into the barracks to lie down for a while. I figured my boats would be back in about an hour. I lay back and began to think how Lt. Rambo could have gotten that information. I couldn't figure it out, and finally just ignored it. Little did I know that within twenty-four hours, the lieutenant's words would be true.

Before the night was over the boats got back and my team came in to see how I was doing. They thought maybe I was hurt worse than I was. I was touched by their concern. But our patrol was not over. We rearmed and refueled the boats, although we took our time doing so. You get real slow when you're back at the base, feeling safe and cozy after having B–40 rockets whiz past your head. We had a big breakfast, too. We weren't afraid to go back; we just didn't want to go back in the dark. We had to go back to the point of contact because that's where the enemy would be, or their bodies if they hadn't already been dragged off. So we piddled around until we knew it would be daylight when we got on station. It must have been nearly 4:00 A.M. when we left the base.

It's not exactly easy to return to the place of an attack because the jungle brush along a river can look the same for miles; there aren't any signs that say you are fifty yards downstream from where you were. You have to hunt for the spot. In the melee of a fire-fight, it's difficult to remember geography; you're just trying to stay alive.

We searched until we were confident we had found the spot of yesterday's attack. If my memory serves me, I was behind the wheel and I beached the boat myself. The captain, Bob, was on the forward part of the deck, directing me where to beach. Then I crawled through the chief's cabin. I ducked down, scooted through toward the bow, and came up right between my guns. I could see a bunker in front of us, about twenty or thirty feet back in the bush. Immediately I spun my guns around, not wanting to leave us unprotected. When you are expecting the enemy, anything looks like movement. I thought I saw movement in that bunker, although I wasn't sure because the brush was so heavy. I did realize, however, that the .50–caliber guns were at the wrong angle to hit the bunker. We weren't under enemy fire, but I was cautious, just knowing that twelve hours before the enemy had been firing rockets at us out of that bunker.

Although I knew the bunker was there, I wasn't sure which opening I was looking at, or if it was, in fact, an open bunker. We were too close to risk throwing a fragmentation grenade; if I missed the hole, I could kill us all. I figured that the right grenade for the job was a white phosphorous grenade, which would do two things: burn down the brush so we could see any booby traps or wires that might be strung around there (I wasn't about to get myself killed just walking up to a bunker to check it out), and give off an intense smoke that would give me some cover while I walked in there to check out the bunker.

The white phosphorous grenade does not look at all like a fragmentation grenade. It is a canister about the size of a soda can, and the trigger (we called it the spoon) runs flat down the side. Even the fragmentation grenades in Vietnam were not like the World War II kind that looked like a pineapple. They were round and smooth, with the spoon on top. When you pull the pin, the spoon would fit down into your hand. And when you threw the grenade, the spoon would fly off. Nothing is activated as long as that spoon is in your hand. You can even reinsert the pin. Inside the fragmentation grenade there are two charges—a small trigger charge and a large charge of explosives surrounded by a compressed stainless steel spring. Every half-inch or so the spring is crimped. When the grenade explodes, the outer casing disintegrates, and the spring breaks at every one of those little indentations. Those little bits of stainless steel can go right through a skull like thousands of razor blades.

I remember carrying in a dead ARVN soldier off the bank of the river one day. I searched that man's body for what killed him, but couldn't for the life of me find a single mark. We helped his buddies strip him to find the death wound. When I turned him over, his head rolled back and his mouth came open, and that's when I saw what had killed him. The roof of his mouth had a tiny mark in it, about half an inch long. Apparently his mouth had been open when a grenade exploded nearby and a piece of steel sliced right through the roof of his mouth into his brain. Not a mark on his body. A little hole in the roof of his mouth, and he was dead.

A white phosphorous grenade, on the other hand, is designed to burn away brush and clear the terrain, to kill the enemy with fire, not shrapnel. The casing will of course blow apart, but it is not designed to disintegrate into small lethal pieces. The TNT charge is the same as in the fragmentation grenades, but the purpose of the explosion is to ignite and spread the phosphorus, which splashes like water. The chemical burns white hot—extremely hot—and one of the by-products of burning white phosphorus is oxygen, so the fire feeds on itself. You can throw a phosphorous grenade in a river and it will still burn. It spreads out and glows, and the water bubbles and boils. We carried those grenades not only to burn away surface vegetation but also to destroy our boats should we be captured or wounded so severely that we couldn't defend them. One grenade will reduce to ashes everything in a radius of about 60 feet.

So I jumped out of the gun tub, grabbed a white phosphorous grenade from the box of ammunition, pulled the pin, and lobbed it toward the bunker. It landed pretty close and started to burn, but it wasn't as effective as I had hoped in clearing away the brush. I figured a second one would finish the job. As I reached for a second grenade, I noticed that a little piece of phosphorus, about the size of a quarter, had come right back and landed in the gun tub. It was burning the fiberglass floor and I hopped down into the gun tub and kicked that piece around with my boot until it burned itself out. While I stood there in the gun tub flipping that bit of phosphorus around with my toe, I thought I might as well throw the second grenade. Everybody was keeping an eye out because we just didn't know yet if the enemy was nearby.

So I stood there in the gun tub, exposed from the armpits up, and pulled the pin on the second grenade. I had drawn my right arm back about six inches from my face, when I heard the explosion. It didn't sound like a firecracker or a bullet or gunfire. I'd never heard anything like it before. It was as if someone had reached up and slapped my ear real hard; first I heard the slap on my ear and then I felt the pressure of the compressed air on my drum. The concussion of the explosion itself was so loud that it deafened me. I heard it and yet almost instantaneously became deaf. I immediately felt heat, but only on the parts of my body not directly covered with phosphorus. I felt no excruciating pain. I just stood there a second, as the ringing grew louder and louder in my right ear. Then there was only silence.

I was wearing my jungle fatigues and my black beret. The beret, made of real thick felt, was blown off my head, but it still protected the top of my head from the initial blast and burning. Above the line of the leather brim, I suffered only second-degree burns. Below that line my facial skin peeled off like a mask and landed right in front of me on the deck of the boat. I looked down and saw half my face on the deck in front of me. Out of my right eye I saw flame, and then nothing more; it went blind. Out of my left eye, I watched as the skin from my face shriveled on the deck like newspaper set aflame. I saw the ashes of my face blow around in a circle, and then float off into the air.

The explosion stripped the skin off the side of my head,

my neck, my right shoulder, the right half of my chest, and my upraised arms.

At first, I thought we had been hit with a rocket. But it quickly dawned on me that my own grenade had exploded. I remained conscious throughout the experience; indeed I remember it with that vivacity peculiar to traumatic moments: Time seems to slow down and the brain, which usually filters out insignificant sensory information, retains every sensation, according significance to each and every one. I saw my skin float away. I felt myself going deaf and blind. I knew my clothes were on fire and that my right hand was severed almost in half. My right thumb was hanging down against my wrist. My skin was literally dripping off me; the skin was white, covered with gobs of burning phosphorus. The moisture in the skin was sucked out and my skin was peeling off. Underneath I saw raw flesh. I recall the smell—of the phosphorus itself and of my own broiling flesh. I had smelled burning flesh, even rotting flesh before, but this had a sweet odor, cloying. I retained my sense of smell, even though the right side of my nose was blown off and all I had left was the left nostril.

I don't remember anybody saying anything, I just knew I had to get out of the gun tub. There was only one way: I had to grab hold of the tops of my .50–caliber guns and hoist myself up, even though I could see that they were glowing red and white from the heat of the explosion. If I had tried to crawl back through underneath the chief's cabin, I would have blown everybody sky high. The ammunition box was there, and I, a living torch, would have ignited the whole cache. As it was, the grenades I had picked from were dangerously hot in their metal boxes at my feet. Incredibly, none exploded. Still phosphorus covered everything. The deck of the boat was on fire.

Still feeling no pain, I grabbed the top of the guns and tried to pull up. I was cooking my palms, but I didn't feel the heat. My hands slipped the first time but I grabbed again, mainly with my left hand, but I still used the palm and index finger of my right. Somehow I pushed myself up, leaned over the left gun, then rolled down onto the deck and into the water. It was the only thing I knew to do.

When I landed in the water, I felt it rushing into my left ear. I could hear the bubbling of my burning skin. Out of my left eye I saw pieces of burning flesh floating up off my chest. But I didn't float. Instead, I drifted under the boat and got pinned between the keel and the river bed. When I felt the crushing pressure of the boat on top of me, I was certain I was going to drown. The thought flashed across my mind, *Brenda is going to be alone again. This time permanently.*

I was face down and being pushed into the mud, but the pressure was against my shoulders and the rest of my body, not against my head. I remember straining and pushing to free myself. It was like a Sumo wrestler was sitting on me. I strained and strained.

Then suddenly the boat came right up off me and I was free. I remember kicking my legs, propelling myself right up from under the boat. When I surfaced, I was facing the boat, but I was on the opposite side from where I had rolled into the water.

My first words after coming up out of the water were, "God, I still believe in You." Those are the exact words. I yelled them. I looked up into the heavens and screamed, "God, I still believe in You" and I think I raised my left fist straight up. I must have been a sight.

I often wonder why those were my first words. In a deep sense that statement represents the powerful influence of my mother in my life. Her attitude toward suffering was always that of Job: "Though [God] slay me, yet will I trust in him." She never blamed God for her afflictions. Somehow I recognized even then that my attitude at that moment—the moment of death—was crucial. I was concerned that God might misunderstand me if I didn't say, *I want You to know, God, that I don't blame You for this.* I didn't want Him to be upset. I didn't want to let Him down. It was both a personal yet respectful statement. At the moment of meeting my Maker, I wanted to be familiar, to call Him *Abba, Pappa,* yet I felt a tremendous fear and awe that required a respectful formality. I had come to Vietnam not asking, "Why me?" I had come asking, "Why not me?" I wanted God to know my attitude hadn't changed; I was still submissive to His will. Of course, I knew that He knew my attitude—I wasn't going to tell God anything that He didn't know—but it seemed as though *I* needed to affirm it for *my* benefit.

I was not fighting doubt. I was just maintaining the communion I had entered into at sixteen with my heavenly Father. My mother's influence shows in that the words I chose were a paraphrase of my mother's faithful cry.

There was a second significance to my cry, "God, I still believe in You." It was a statement also addressed to my buddies in defense of God. That may sound presumptuous—defending the ways of God to men in such a moment—but I didn't want to let them say, "Look what Roever's God did to him."

We had a brand new guy on board who had been in Vietnam only a few days. When he saw me come up, still bubbling and glowing, he leaped into the water and swam right up to me. I remember the bizarre look on his face: It was as though he had suddenly discovered war really is hell; he had been dropped into an inferno, and his horrified expression seemed to say, *This is going to happen to us all.* I did a turn in the water and started swimming an overhand crawl. I remember my finger flopping and my skin, large chunks of which had become detached, floating away with the current as so much refuse.

That rookie followed me, bless his heart, swimming after me through fragments of my burning flesh. He kept reaching for me and yet stopped short of doing so; he would have caught on fire himself. When I got to the riverbank, my feet sank deep in the mud. I kept pushing against the mud but I didn't know if I would have the strength to stand up or whether I would fall back in the water and die.

I wanted to get out of the water. I was sure I would drown if I didn't. I was willing to die on the bank of the river but not in the water. I had realized by then that in or out of the water, I would continue to burn. I wasn't afraid to die, but I didn't want to drown.

By this time a more exact quotation from the Scriptures had come to mind. It was Paul's statement in Philippians, "To die is gain." In my mind I began saying over and over, "To die is gain, to die is gain." I thought I was going to die, but death didn't present any threat.

Life did. When I got up on the bank of the river I realized that God was telling me I wasn't going to die. He reminded me of the first half of that verse: "For to me to live is Christ." Over and over and over I was saying, "To die is gain" and yet I began hearing, like an echo, "To live is Christ." To die is gain, to live is Christ. Suddenly I understood that my apparent submission to God's will was shot through with a faithless wish to die. Subconsciously I wanted to die. I was much more afraid of what life would be like after the explosion than death. I couldn't see the full extent of my injuries, but I knew I was more of a mess than Larry's "trophy." I had seen my own face, my own skin, and with them my own identity, turn to ashes and drift away in the light breeze. When I said, "God, I still believe in You," it was as though I were trying to say, *Forget "to live is Christ"; I believe in You so let me die.*

Now I know all these thoughts and feelings happened within the course of a few seconds, but this conversation with God was taking place in the deepest part of my spirit. And in those moments of debate between God and me, I came to know something of how Paul felt when he said, "I am in a strait betwixt two, having a desire to depart, and to be with Christ; which is far better: nevertheless to abide in the flesh is more needful for you." Through the little dialogue that took place over the two halves of that verse, it was as though God were saying, *I understand your desire to be with me, to escape the torment of recovery. But you must understand My desire. My use for you is not over.*

As the two halves of that verse called to one another I realized that to live in Christ from then on was going to be a kind of living death. "To live is Christ," but to live in Christ is to die to the self and to be crucified with Him—to be baptized by fire and water into His death before rising up from that baptism into His resurrection. And in many respects my life has been a living death for fifteen years. And as soon as I get callous to that fact—as soon as I begin to think that "to live is Roever," as soon as I start to get self-satisfied and begin to think that my ministry owes its success to my charisma, to my power and beauty—God reminds me that "to live is Christ." He reminds me that such a life is a crucifixion, a continual bearing of Christ's cross, a wearing of Christ's torn flesh just as He wore ours, a life of sharing the mockery and ridicule and scornful laughter borne by Christ on the cross. We are to be "crucified with Christ."

I'm still learning the lesson I began to learn on that muddy riverbank in Vietnam: that the Christian life is a dying to self, it's an ongoing crucifixion of one's own will. Deep in my spirit, I must have sensed, even then, as I watched my flesh bubble and burn on that riverbank, that my disfigurement would keep me hanging on a cross. In rolling into the water and coming up on the other side of the boat, I had undergone a baptism of water and fire and blood into the death of Christ. I had gone under that water with one identity and come up with another. Stripped of my own skin, my own face, I emerged clothed in Christ in a new way. I experienced in the flesh what every believer must learn: one must be stripped and clothed in Christ, but before one can be clothed in Christ's glory, one must wear the clothes of His shame. In this each Christian recapitulates, in a small way, the action of Christ's incarnation; for He was stripped of His heavenly glory and clothed in corruptible human flesh so that our flesh might become incorruptible.

Splashing, burning, bleeding, I managed to pull myself

out of the mud and lean back on my haunches. There, crouched on the bank, I had a peculiar vision that may seem comical and irrelevant, particularly in the context of the foregoing theological reflections. It was not a vision of Jesus or anything spiritual, but one of my guitar. My folks had bought me a brand new Gibson twelve-string electric guitar as a going-away gift. The whole time I was in Vietnam one of my daydreams was about going home to play that guitar. In my vision I saw that guitar on a stand right in front of me. I said, *Guitar, I will play you again.* I had just looked at my wounded hands and yet I said, *Guitar, I will play you again.* The Spirit of God gave me hope. In the midst of the greatest defeat of my life, there appeared this apparition of good things to come. Then suddenly I fell over backwards, and everybody thought I had died.

As I lay on my back, the phosphorus continued to burn into my chest cavity. A lot of the phosphorus had dripped off with my skin, but some had seeped down into my body. A hole burned right through the little cavity above the sternum into the trachea, and I began to breathe through my chest. At the same time I felt as if I were suffocating. My cheek was almost completely blown off, my jawbone was charred black and sticking out and my teeth were visible. My tongue had become so swollen that it stuffed the cavity of my mouth and more. I tried to speak but nothing would come out. I had not yet felt pain, but of course I was in shock. I had no proper sense of time. If I recall, the guys gathered around me in a circle, one of them was packing mud on me to try to stop the burning and Pervert Number Two was kneeling over me, praying. Bob was lying beside me. His face, arms, and hands were burned to the second degree. The phosphorus had set his clothes on fire, and jumping in the water had saved his life. I never did know how the two of us ended up so close together on that riverbank.

I must have lapsed in and out of consciousness, because the next thing I remember is hearing the whipping sound of the helicopter blades and thinking how fast the dust-off had gotten there. The mud had not put out the fire, and I was still burning when the helicopter landed. They rolled me onto the stretcher, face down, thinking I was dead. They carried Bob over first because he was still alive, and then came back for me. In the meantime, I had caught the stretcher on fire, and when they picked it up, it ripped open and I fell out on my head. Then they rolled me up in wet blankets to suppress the flames. My skin was so dehydrated, it was like burning paper.

I was barely conscious and remember little of being lifted out. I know the medic on the chopper thought I was dead. When I tried to call out "Medic," the poor guy went bonkers. He thought I had come back to life. I said "Medic" because I was afraid he might stick my dogtags into my gums. That was the usual procedure with the dead. If the dogtags hang around your neck, they might break off and get lost; then you're unidentifiable. So when someone dies, they drive his dogtags up between his teeth and gums and then they stay put. There I was, about blown in half, but still conscious enough not to want my gums split. The medic was going crazy, and the pilot tried to get him to shut up and settle down. Now, I can't be sure about this, but I remember feeling as though the pilot lost control of the chopper. The back end swung around, the chopper dropped, and I felt weightless. I remember thinking, *Oh God, we're going to crash, and I'll be the only survivor.* Black humor perhaps, and yet it shows how I had begun to believe, no matter what happened, that I was going to live. I was not going to die. I had accepted it.

I begged for water. They couldn't give me any, but finally let me have little pieces of ice.

The medic tried to get some morphine into me, and I vaguely recall that he had problems—he couldn't find a needle for the syringe and finally just stuck the syringe itself into a wound in my leg and pumped the stuff in. It didn't do any good. When the helicopter landed and I was unloaded, the wind whipped up by the blades was just like a bellows blowing hot coals, and I burst into flames again. Then I started to feel the pain.

While I was in transport, the verse "To live is Christ, to die is gain" began to mix with a phrase from a secular song, "Walk like a man, my son" until the rhythm of my mind was "To live is Christ, to die is gain; walk like a man, my son. To live is Christ, to die is gain; walk like a man, my son." Those phrases ran through my mind for days. They speak little of the spiritual battles to come, the mixture of spiritual lessons to be learned and the machismo habits of the mind I had to unlearn.

That chopper flew me to a MASH unit, the Third Field Hospital. We arrived there on the date of my injury, July 26, 1969. The first job was to get the fire out. They scraped it out of me, cutting my burning flesh away. Some of it had blasted deep into me, and as they would cut out burned and blackened flesh, they would expose more phosphorus which would burst into flame when it hit oxygen. (Incredible as it may sound, chunks of phosphorus were still smoking twelve days later when they opened me up in Texas.) They cleaned up the hole that had been burned in my trachea, inserted a plastic tube, and I breathed through that hole for almost a year. They gave me massive amounts of morphine, but that didn't stop the incredible pain I began to feel.

I remember hearing part of a conversation that was not meant for my ears. One doctor said, "He's not going to make it." The guy on my right said, "I think we ought to try." The first guy thought they should spend their energy on the wounded who had a chance. The guy on the right said, "Let's at least go ahead and get the fire out." I felt like God and the Devil were bargaining for my soul. Obviously the guy on the right won.

I stayed in the Third Field Hospital two and a half days. They cleaned me up as best they could and put out the fire. Then they loaded me back on the chopper which took me to Tan Son Nhut air field in Saigon. There an ambulance transported me to the nearby hospital, and, incredibly, the ambulance stalled in heavy afternoon traffic. I recall lying in oppressive, suffocating heat, with nobody tending me, until the drivers eventually got the engine started.

I was held at the Tan Son Nhut Hospital only one night, then shipped off to Japan where sophisticated burn treatment could begin. I remember hardly anything of the night in Saigon. Thanks to the drugs, I don't remember any pain, just voices and activity.

The next morning, hooked to an IV and still asking for water, I began the trip to Japan. My stretcher was rolled out to a big hospital transport plane where I joined a long line of wounded soldiers on stretchers waiting to be stacked inside. We were on our way out of Nam. And though we were leaving the war behind, we still had battles to fight. Some would win, others would not. But none of us would ever be the same.

12

I arrived at the 106th General Hospital in Yokohama, Japan, on July 29, 1969. A woman from the Red Cross came by to help me write a letter to my family. She wasn't real tactful in suggesting something in the nature of a final good-bye. I could have kicked her out of the room, but I have to admit that reason was on her side. There wasn't much cause for hope.

From the waist up I had suffered massive damage: approximately 40 percent third-degree burns. I was fortunate to have thrown the grenade from down in the gun tub, which protected me from the waist down. Except for a few places on my leg where my trousers had caught fire, my legs and my lower trunk were not burned at all. If I had been standing up and holding the grenade, the phosphorus would have coated the entire right side of my body, and I probably would have died right there.

At the time of my injury I weighed 190 pounds. Now I was 130. I'd lost sixty pounds of flesh and body fluids. The deepest burns were on the right side of my face under my chin and on my neck, not only from the blast and the phosphorus, but from my burning clothes.

I was placed on a bed that revolved vertically through a full circle, something like the giant wheel to which the expert knife thrower's assistant is attached. While she spins around, he throws his knives, outlining her limbs in dramatic fashion. In my case, the revolutions took place very slowly, once an hour or so; this measure was taken because a burn victim is subject to fluids filling his lungs, slowly diminishing respiration until cardiac arrest takes place. And instead of throwing the knives around me, they used them on me, debriding (pronounced "debreeding") or cutting away my flesh as it continued to die.

My moment of blackest despair occurred in Japan. A medic was foolish enough to grant my request for a mirror. He held it up in front of me—one of those magnifying mirrors, no less.

When I looked in that mirror, I saw a monster, not a human being, certainly not Dave Roever. My face was covered with charred black skin, and swollen on the left side almost to the width of my shoulders. My left eye—the one I could see out of—seemed to bug out of its socket.

And the right side? It was nearly flat; a few scraps of dead flesh hung by their sinews from the bones of my skull. Liquid oozed from the flesh that was left. There were a few pouches of swelling where the flesh still had circulation, but for the most part my cheek had been blown clean away. It opened up down through my lower gums to my chin, way back to the muscle. I could look clear inside my head. My gums were charred. My teeth were black. My tongue was still swollen, filling the mouth cavity. I had no right ear at all, no hair, and I could see patches of exposed bone all over my head, especially above my ear and at my brow. The right half of my nose was gone; I had only one nostril. My right eye was gray and lacked an eyelid—just a big gray eyeball sitting there.

I also got a glimpse of the gaping hole in my chest. I could see the bumps on my esophagus, the tendons in my throat. I could see my ribs, I could see organs moving around inside of me. Everything looked wet. The three outside fingers on my right hand were almost severed. Only one finger on my right hand was still attached—my index finger was undamaged, not even burned.

When I looked into that mirror I was struck with a lightning bolt of soul-destroying pain. I can tell you that the pain of being burned is a shriveling pain that makes you feel like you're being sucked into the air about you, which in a way you are, and that brings with it a visceral knowledge of pure extinction, nonbeing. The pain I felt when I looked in that mirror was similar, but worse. My soul seemed to shrivel up, to collapse in on itself, to be sucked into a black hole of despair. I was left with an indescribable and terrifying emptiness. I was alone in the way the souls in hell must feel alone. Jesus used the words of the psalmist when He cried, "My God, my God, why hast thou forsaken me?" The pitch and timbre of his voice registered in my own feelings of desertion.

When the medic walked away I reached over, wrapped my little finger around the tube going into me and yanked that thing out. I assumed it was my life-line, filling me perhaps with the blood on which my life depended. I lay there waiting to die, wanting to die, but nothing happened except I began to feel hungry. I had pulled out the tube feeding me!

I've never known despair as I did in those moments. The time I got drunk was a bright sunny day in comparison. I was overwhelmed by fears of rejection. I found myself utterly repulsive. I could not and would not identify myself with the monster in the mirror. How could anybody else?

My thoughts and fears centered in Brenda. I was stricken with fear that my wife would be ashamed of me. I couldn't imagine that she could love me, play beauty to the beast I had become. *If I live through this,* I thought, *I will be a freak. She is a young woman, barely twenty years old; too young to be stuck with somebody like me.* These thoughts may sound magnanimous, but they were largely selfish, because the worst possibility would have been the fulfillment of this logic, seeing my young wife walking away with another man, arm in arm. Somebody would come along who could give her better than I could, and she'd take it.

What could anybody do with a life like mine? My lifetime of dreaming about being an evangelist burned to ashes and drifted away in that light wind. Perhaps I could hook on with one of the touring freak shows: See the fat lady, see the hermaphrodite, see the Siamese twins preserved in formaldehyde, see Roever.

I was loaded with drugs and, despite their effects, experiencing an almost hallucinatory state of agony—I have to consider these mitigating factors when assessing my guilt for attempting suicide. I was responsible ultimately, but, to be sure, I had lost my good judgment through circumstances beyond, way beyond, my control. I will have to wait until eternity to have it judged as God alone can judge it. In the immediate sphere of the temporal, far from punishing me, He was rushing special graces my way.

God was taking care of me, typically enough, through my mother. In the very hour of my injury, which was the middle of the night state-side, my mother sat bolt upright in bed with a tremendous urgency from God to pray. When my dad was awakened by the intensity of her praying, Mom said, "It's David." Together they continued to pray. I believe those prayers meant the difference between life and death for me.

When my family received official word of my injury, Mom was able to reach Paul Klahr, a missionary stationed in Japan, by phone and said, "I have a son over there who's been severely injured. He's not expected to live. Would you please try to find him and just go comfort him and pray with him?" He was on his way immediately. He found me on my third day in Japan and walked through the door not twenty minutes after I had attempted suicide. When I was at my lowest, I saw him walk up to me like an angel sent from heaven. I looked at this guy and said, "You are a Christian, aren't you?" (I had never seen that man in my life.)

He said, "Yes, I am. I've come to pray for you."

I grinned and said, "Hallelujah." He started praying for me, and I fell sound asleep. Sound asleep. My healing began while I slept. I woke up ready to live.

I was flown from Japan to Randolph Air Force Base. From there I was transported in a convoy of ambulances to Brooke Army Medical Center at Fort Sam Houston in San Antonio, Texas, where I spent four weeks in an intensive care unit and another eight months in the burn ward for skin transplant operations.

Thirteen of us, all burn victims, arrived together and were placed in intensive care, Ward 14A. A couple of guys were already in there. I remember seeing one sitting up in an old-timey wooden wheelchair, with all his skin burned off. He looked like living hamburger meat. They were trying to feed him scrambled eggs, but he couldn't keep anything down. He died soon after we arrived.

I had been wrapped in bandages for the trip, yards and yards of bandages. Their first job was unwrapping me, which took maybe a half hour or an hour. When they pulled off the bandages, gobs of junk came off with them. As soon as they were done, they allowed me to see Brenda—and Brenda to see me.

Brenda and her folks and my folks were all there waiting, but for the first visit, only Brenda came in. I had felt wrapped in the arms of God since Paul Klahr's visit, and I longed to see Brenda. Yet I felt tremendous anxiety, too, as if the tracheotomy hadn't been performed and I was suffocating once more. I waited for her to walk through the door, wondering how she would react when she saw me, wondering what the expression on her face would be, wondering if she could accept me. I felt as though my whole future, my whole identity, my life itself depended on the look on her face when she saw me.

The nurses tried to prepare both patients and loved ones

for these unhappy reunions. Few of us were expected to live. Few of us did. We were all grossly disfigured. Monsters. The nurses didn't walk our loved ones straight up to us. They took them the long way around and showed them other patients first, so that the husband or son in question would not present the shock he otherwise might. I imagined Brenda thinking, *Thank God, that's not my husband,* until the thought dawned on her, *maybe my husband will look worse.* Nothing totally prepares people for the sight of burn victims.

When Brenda walked in, she was gorgeous, more beautiful than I had ever seen her. She had a hospital gown on, but I could see she had dressed up for her man. In an instant, I saw that she had remained absolutely faithful to me, that she had lived for me, and kept herself chaste for me during those months of separation. The memory of her love had warned me off all temptations; it had kept me from violating her trust, and, somehow, my first feeling upon seeing her was of her worthiness, her fidelity. She was absolutely worthy of the virtue, the chastity, she had inspired in me. She was beautiful, possessed of an inner radiance which came from her relationship with God.

Brenda walked straight up to my bed, paused at the chart, and looked right at me. Showing not the slightest tremor of horror or shock, she bent down and kissed me on what was left of my face. Then she looked me in my good eye, smiled, and said, "Welcome home, Davey. I love you." To understand what that meant to me you have to know that's what she called me when we were most intimate; she would whisper "Davey" over and over in my ear. By calling me Davey, by invoking and embracing once more the intimacy of her knowledge of me, she said exactly what I needed to know. By using her term of endearment for me, she said, *You are my husband. You will always be my husband. You are still my man.* That word of tender intimacy was a creative word of perfect love which cast out my fears.

All I could say was, "I want you to know I'm real sorry."
She said, "Why are you sorry?"

"Because I always wanted to look good for you. Now I can never look good for you again."

She grinned and said, "Oh Davey, you never were good looking anyway." And that was the beginning of the deep psychological and spiritual healing which eventually quenched the fire of my ordeal, at least enough for me to face the world again.

She left there, I think, just as quickly as she came. They wouldn't let our loved ones stay long. We were still recovering from the trauma of being moved. My body was still just trying to survive. But when Brenda left, the confidence was there, and I knew everything was going to be all right between us.

How could that woman love me so much? How could she look at a creature composed of inflammation and charred bone and yet look as though I were the man of her dreams come home? Only God could put it in a woman to love a man the way she did. Through His mercy He placed the knowledge of my true self, the person made in God's image, deep within her heart. To paraphrase an old hymn, His grace befriended her outward sight, and made her inner vision clear.

God loves us in our putrid condition of sin, and Brenda had a Christlike love for me. She imitated Christ in helping Him accomplish the redemptive work of putting me back together—which is what God is trying to do for us all. He is trying to restore us from the freakish condition of being sinners, from all that it means to be mortal, to being once more the supernatural and immortal creature God made in Adam, which we can be in glory through believing in the midst of our often grotesque world in the last Adam, Jesus Christ. The surest evidence I have of the love of Christ is in the love my wife showed me. When she stood up after that first kiss, her gorgeous lips were covered with my own dead skin. She was a type of Christ—the immortal God who put on our mortality, our dead flesh—smiling at me, in agony, from the cross.

That day Brenda gently began to lead me from being an Old Testament Christian, someone committed to obeying God's Law perfectly, to a New Testament Christian, someone who obeys the law out of his love for a person, Christ Jesus. My models would change from Samson and the Old Testament prophets, who were possessed of the strength of their righteousness, to the powerless figure of the Virgin Mary, whose strength was nothing but the power and strength of God Himself when she said, "Be it unto me according to thy word."

13

My first few days at Brooke the staff was intent on one thing: keeping me alive. They were thinking survival, not skin grafts. They didn't even change the sheets until my vital signs began to stabilize. My veins were collapsing, and they had trouble keeping the intravenous hook-ups in place. They'd stick a needle through the charred rubble trying to find a vein, and I mean they'd stick it in there and wiggle it around. They went to the back of my hand; they went to my forehead; they went, finally, to my feet.

Once, when they were trying to hook an IV into a vein in the groin, the needle broke off in there. The nurse hit the "emergency" buzzer and a doctor and several nurses came running. She said, "The tube is broken off in his groin. I'm afraid it's in the vein."

The doctor grabbed a knife and just cut in, no anesthetic or anything. I grabbed the bed—here I am a bloody mess anyway—and gritted my teeth, my eyes rolling up in my head, while he reached in there with his fingers and pulled it out. They stitched up the vessel and then stitched up my thigh.

Taking in enough liquid (and, later on, food) was a big deal. Skin acts as an insulation to hold body heat in, and when a person has lost 40 percent of that skin, as I had, the body heat escapes like heat out of a chimney. In that state, I burned up calories at a tremendous rate. I stayed hooked up to an IV bottle for a long time. At first when they started giving me food, I couldn't eat. I had no appetite and began to lose more weight, my muscles atrophying.

The doctors came in one day with a big tray of food and ganged up on me—about three of them. "Doesn't that look good? You're going to eat it all."

I said, "I'll try."

One of them replied, "No, you *will*. If you want out of this hospital alive, you'll have to eat your way out the front door. You eat or you die." They kept high-calorie foods and liquids in front of me constantly. They served me a two-quart pitcher of a black chocolate malt drink with every meal. I had to drink every bit of it.

Brenda was a tremendous help at this stage. Every day she came to the hospital and fed me like a baby. There were times when I was so doped up with pain killers that I would forget to chew the spoonful she had just shoveled into my mouth. She was patience itself; she never became frustrated: "chew" she would remind me, and I would refocus my attention on eating. Later, she would bring in hamburgers, candy bars, Dairy Queen malts, and pizzas to supplement the hospital's own offerings. (The meals the hospital served me were as bad as hospital meals everywhere, despite their crucial significance.)

For much of the time I only had half of my mouth open—the other half closed by skin grafts—and I would be frustrated by not being able to take a big bite of one of those hamburgers. Brenda thought of a way to satisfy even this desire; she cut the hamburgers up in small pieces and helped me stuff my cheek full of them so that I could have the satisfaction of taking a big bite. Somehow receiving this kind of help from Brenda was less shameful for me than receiving it from the nurses. Her presence aided and encouraged my appetite so that I consumed all the calories my body needed in its efforts to recover.

I went in for my first operation under general anesthesia

on August 8, 1969. I could hardly believe the surgeon's report; my right hand was still smoking from the phosphorus: "Upon opening the wound for inspection, there was obvious smoke coming from the wound and during the course of debridement five phosphorous particles were removed from the wound."

According to the surgeons and a ballistics expert, a sniper's bullet must have penetrated my hand from the back and ignited the grenade. If that's the case, it's clear that he was firing from behind us on the opposite side of the river. I understand, however, that there are also reports of phosphorous grenades exploding prematurely. Recently I saw my old boat captain. He thinks the grenade was faulty. If a sniper's bullet was the cause, the angles suggest that if my hand hadn't been up, the bullet would have hit me in the head. And I know I would rather be a living freak than a dead corpse.

Those summer and autumn months were full of constant and indescribable pain. When you put your hand on a hot stove burner, the actual burning sensation is like a jolt, not a lasting tingling feeling, but a sudden shock that makes you jerk your hand away. Well, I felt that shock all through my body: a bolt of pain that stays with you and stays with you and stays with you. There's no way to jerk away from it. You roll, toss, turn, stick to the sheets—my back was burnt too and I would stick to the sheet—but I couldn't escape the pain.

When I sat up, gobs of bloody pulp stuck to the sheets—an experience not too far from being skinned alive.

Morning sponge baths and sheet changes were torture. When the guy came soon after, about eight o'clock, to take X-rays with his portable machine, he would say, "Skinning time. I know it hurts. I'm sorry."

Yet that pain was a mild preliminary to what followed each morning: the torture of being "tanked" and "buttered," as both patients and nurses called it. Every morning we were soaked in a stainless steel tank, like a cross-shaped bath tub in which you could lie flat, arms outstretched, for "debridement," the sloughing away and cutting off of dead skin and tissue.

Deteriorating flesh can poison you. Part of your own flesh, if it is dying, will become infested with bacteria and kill you. The tank was filled with antibacterial saline solutions both to combat infection and to restore vital natural salts to the body. The bath itself stung and burned like fire. But then, like the demons in one of the levels of Dante's inferno, the nurses would go to work with big pincers and cut away the dead or dying flesh. Some of it was so dead it would just pull away. But they always cut on the living side of the tissue. I don't recall anything ever coming off that didn't hurt.

Psychological pain was added to the physical torture when it came to cutting up on my face. A piece of my nose remained that would never have life in it again. I was born with that nose, and in an instant it was gone. The nurse reached down, lifted up half my nose, and clip, there it went. They also cut away what was left of my right eyelid. Part of it I saw burn on the deck, but one flap remained. It was dead, so, clip. It's not easy to watch parts of your body being cut away and tossed in the garbage.

Despite the morphine they gave us to lessen the pain, the hospital sounded like a torture chamber during debriding time. And because of the screaming, they never let visitors in while we were being "tanked."

We received our shots of morphine at a regular time before debridement, and eventually I noticed that some of the guys got to looking forward to the debriding. When you start looking forward to pain so you can take drugs, something is wrong. That's where I drew the line. One day—August 17 to be precise, I refused the pretank medication. "I don't want the shot," I said. But the male nurse didn't pay any attention to me and just kept on rolling up the sleeve of my gown. I said again, "I don't want this shot, and you're not going to stick me with that needle."

"Roever," he said, "that's not like you. You've never been any trouble. You always cooperate."

I said, "I'm cooperating with you now. But you will not put that needle in me."

He called the doctor, and I explained my reasoning, "I've been watching some of the guys," I told him, "and they seem to like those shots more and more every day. I'd rather leave here dead than leave here hooked on drugs."

He was somewhat skeptical but said, "Well, let's see how far you can go with it."

The woman doing the work on me didn't know I hadn't been given my shot. When she pulled that first chunk off me, I yelled, "Oh, God," like I'd never yelled before. The pain was something wild. She looked at me and said, "Young man, there will be no cursing or splashing of water in this tank."

"Don't you know the difference between cursing and praying?" I gasped. But I gritted my teeth and never again uttered a sound. The pain was so intense that tears rolled down my cheek.

I would go up into that tank and every muscle in my body would tremble from pain. I would bow my body upwards, letting only the back of my head and the backs of my heels touch the tank, trying to escape the pain. They had to push me down to keep the water over me. But I never went back to the morphine.

After we were "tanked" we were "buttered" with silver nitrate cream to fight infection. Keeping us sterile was of course a big concern. When you are burned, your body is an open sepulchre for every strain of bacteria that floats in the air and lands on the body. Many of these strains can cause lethal infections. The kidneys of a burn victim are often overworked by the job of cleaning away the toxins in his system—kidney failure is a frequent cause of death. We called the silver nitrate "white lightning" as well as "butter," because it would sting and burn with a shocking intensity that knocked the wind out of us. But after the flamelike stinging subsided, a numbness would set in that made the pain much more tolerable. We hated that butter and loved it, too.

Every day, as I've mentioned, from the minute the doors were opened to visitors until five minutes after they were closed, Brenda was by my side. She was the last one to leave. They had to run her out. While other wives fought unsuccessfully to hide their embarrassment and their feelings of revulsion toward the "monsters" in front of them, Brenda was as openly affectionate as she could be. Even in a busy intensive care burn ward, there were moments of privacy where Brenda's presence and affection transported me for a short time away from the constant pain and horror of my injuries. She was there serving me, when other wives were serving up divorce papers. Burn victims are often impotent and almost always rendered sterile from the trauma the body sustains. But Brenda reawakened what might have remained long dormant. Her constant companionship and the expression of her love for me rekindled my own desires for her, a great sign of health and healing, both psychologically and physically.

Brenda carried on a running joke with the doctor. Every day, when she was sure I would hear her, she would say, "Doctor, may I take him home tonight?"

He'd say, "Miss Brenda, you know better than that."

After hearing the request repeatedly, one day the doctor asked, "What are you going to do with him?"

She answered, "Why I'll do more for him in one night than you'll do for him in a year."

Brenda got an apartment in San Antonio, and my parents drove down from Fort Worth as often as possible. They knew I was in good hands with Brenda. I belonged to her. They treated me as Brenda's husband first, and as their son second. They saw that she was God's chief conduit of grace to me.

Many people came to visit me, especially pastor friends of my father's, and I was grateful for their taking time to come see me. But they would often make what I might call a "pastoral" mistake in relating my injuries to something they had experienced, or other cases they had known about. Someone in the kind of pain I was in doesn't want the singular identity of what he is experiencing belittled. Comparisons always tend to diminish the integrity of the experience, depriving it of its legitimate status as something unique.

The person who had the greatest right to make a comparison never did. That was my mother. My mother's life had been and would continue to be defined by suffering in much the same way as mine. But she never said, "Now, Son, I've been there. And here's what you are going to have to do." Yet her visits, except for Brenda's, were the most helpful to me. Without words, beyond them, it was as though we shared an inside scoop on the inscrutable mystery of the ways of God. She strengthened my spirit by her example; the long years of suffering had tempered her spirit and taught her much about patience and prayer. (In her later years, until her death a year ago, I think my presence soothed and strengthened her spirit in much the same way.)

Brenda's spirit ministered to mine in a similar fashion. Although she had never undergone a prolonged illness, her fidelity and her attitude of sacrificial love and the practice of it had given her a wisdom well beyond her years and deeper, much deeper, than I could fathom. The three of us composed a community of suffering, which knew something of what the apostle Paul spoke of when he counted it a privilege to "fill out" the sufferings of Christ.

My fourteen months of hospitalization can be divided into three phases, although they overlap somewhat. For the first month or so, my survival was at stake. I didn't know what lay ahead; I didn't know how to think about the future; and I was in agonizing pain.

A psychological turning point came on September 3 when I was taken off what we would commonly call the critical list: my official status changed from Very Seriously Ill to Seriously Ill. Thus began the long six-month middle phase of my recovery, punctuated by fourteen major skin graft operations. These had begun a few days after I arrived at Brooke hospital on August 4. I was removed from the Seriously Ill list on October 10, and had two thirty-day convalescent leaves from mid-October to mid-November and from Christmas to the end of January 1970.

The last phase, when my recovery was certain and I could begin looking ahead to life outside the hospital, may be dated from March 10, when I was finally taken out of the intensive care ward for specialized burn treatment and transferred to the regular burn ward. During April, I had a third thirty-day convalescent leave, and a month later I was transferred to the VA hospital in Dallas, closer to home, for a final four months of recovery, largely as a self-caring patient, until my official discharge in September 1970.

The long, tedious, painful period of fourteen operations demanded that I summon once more the internal fortitude that had allowed me to withstand the physical ordeals of training on Mare Island and the psychological stress of the POW training on Whidbey Island. For indeed, I was now a prisoner as I had never been before, and my jailer was pain, pure physical suffering. Pain usually places you in solitary confinement, it's one lonely place. But, as I recount the specifics of this purgatorial period, remember that Brenda and my mother were by my side. Those two women knew how to sing in the dark; they filled my jail of pain with singing as Paul and Silas had filled theirs. And because Brenda and my mother were there for me, *with* me, I was not alone. In fact, Brenda's touch, as it communicated her love for me, seemed to take away or rather take unto herself part of my suffering. There was something in this of "bearing one another's burdens" that was not merely metaphorical but quite literal: in a real sense she was afflicted with my infirmities in the depths of her soul. Her love enveloped that pain and brought gladness into a time of excruciating pain. I started to learn how to sing in the dark myself.

Skin grafting occurs in different stages. First you get grafts of animal skin, called *hemografts*. As your body tries to grow that skin, blood vessels move to the surface of your injury. But the body finally can't accept the animal skin, so the graft eventually dies. In the meantime, however, those blood vessels have started preparing the area for new layers of skin. The grafted area gets a lot of bloody fluid under it and then floats off.

The next graft stage is called *homografts* and makes use of skin that people donate like other body organs. For a while I had some guy's tattoo right on my face. I was the pride of the ward. These can be laid on without anesthesia and are held in place by dressings.

After the homograft, your body is ready for *autograft,* the final stage of grafts; these are taken from your own body. My series of operations involved replacing homograft with autograft, and then replacing portions of autograft that didn't successfully "take" the first time.

There are actually two different processes involved in getting one's own skin to grow on parts of one's body that have suffered third-degree burns. In skin grafting, as such, skin is taken from one part of the body and placed somewhere else. Seven layers of cells make up the epidermis. You can burn off six of them and still have enough skin to grow back, although if you even touch that last layer, it will rub off because it's so fragile. But if it's undamaged, it can produce a full layer of skin.

To get skin for an autograft, they use a small razorlike machine, called a "Brown dermatome," that works like a wood-plane to lift off three or four of those six layers of skin at a controlled thickness of eight to ten thousandths of an inch. They'd press that razor down and drag it across your body, and your skin would roll right up on it. A second later, the blood would pop right up out of your pores. Then they scrape off another row beside the first. My thighs, which is where they lifted most of the skin for autograft, look like zebra skin.

In the second process, called *skin culturing,* a roll of skin is pinched together from an undamaged area of the body, but it is kept attached to the body at both ends. The loop remains alive and resembles a handle on a suitcase. Then the surgeon can separate one end of the loop, shift that piece to a nearby area that needs new skin, and stitch it in place.

Repairing my face and head was the most difficult and delicate surgical task, as a summary of my operations, with a little help from the medical records, indicates. On August 14, homograft was removed from the right side of my face, neck, upper chest, and right hand and replaced with auto-graft taken from my thighs. The first of the new skin was applied to my right eye, from which new eyelids would be constructed. (My upper and lower right eyelids were sewn shut.) Surgery on August 18 did much the same thing: re-placing more homograft with autograft on my face, neck, chest, arm, and left and right hands. On August 26, my left thumb was amputated at the "interphalangeal joint," and more delicate work was performed on my right eye toward making grafted skin into eyelids. On September 3 my status was changed from Very Seriously Ill to Seriously Ill, and on September 8, the surgeon did further work on my eyelid with grafts taken from my left arm and more repair work on my right ear area; also autograft was placed on my left thumb stump.

The surgeon's report says, the operative procedure of

September 25 was cancelled when I "developed airway obstruction" as I was being given anesthesia. I "developed profound bradycardia" and had a "period of cardiac arrest." That is, apparently as a result of an allergic reaction to the anesthesia, my larynx collapsed and my heart stopped. From then on the surgeons were cautious about using general anesthesia and switched whenever possible to local anesthesia.

On October 2, further repair work was done on my left thumb; on the sixth, a graft from the right side of my stomach was used to continue the reconstruction of my right upper eyelid. On October 10, I was removed from the Seriously Ill list—another turning point—and given a weekend pass, which was extended, after a check-up on the twelfth, to a thirty-day convalescent leave.

Going home to Brenda for our first night together remains the most precious moment of my life. Brenda guaranteed my healing when she said, "Welcome home, Davey," but that guarantee was sealed and my healing largely performed when she took me into her arms that night. She had worked very hard to make everything perfect, I'm telling you. In fact, she wore the evening gowns and lingerie she had prepared to wear on our R and R vacation in Hawaii, which was to have taken place the week after my injury.

I was afraid that I would never be able to put out of my mind my own horrible ugliness. And I could scarcely imagine that Brenda would be able to see beyond that ugliness. But that special evening cast out every fear I had. Alone for the first time since I had gone off to Vietnam, together on our own marriage bed in our own apartment, there was great spiritual and emotional healing.

I wanted that woman so much! It was as though I was able to say to Brenda, *I love you, and I am still the man you married, and I am still the husband who took you home that first night, when we were both virgins.* That night was as passionate and innocent as our first night of love because we had remained chaste during our separation. I felt confirmed by the Spirit in my resistance to the temptations of the flesh which the Devil had set before me in Vietnam. I felt this renewed intimacy was God's blessing on our fidelity. That night Brenda and I consummated our love as though we had never had the privilege in our marriage before, thus beginning the next stage in the process of my healing. In the hospital Brenda's love had to be confined to her presence, her words, brief kisses, and the touch of her hand; but when she could present herself, body and soul, and yield to me—embracing me and accepting my embrace—only Jesus knows the full extent of how that night has shaped my destiny.

The beauty of Christ's love for the church is that He loves the church even in its ugliness. Saint Paul tells the husband to love his wife as Christ loves the church, so I'm reversing the roles of the analogy here, but Brenda loved me the way Christ loves the church, even in its ugliness, embracing it as though it were the most beautiful bride in the world. It's His embrace that makes the church holy, and Brenda's embrace that made me feel worthy, a man with his dignity intact.

When I had looked into that mirror in Japan, I felt subhuman; I felt like an animal. I could not see the image of God in my reflection. In my training on Whidbey Island when the specially trained officers' corp impersonated the North Vietnamese, the enemy tried to make you into an animal, to make you nothing but a creature with animal appetites, to arouse a man's appetite so much that he would forget his ideals. In a sense, my buddies in Vietnam played exactly the same game. They wanted me to become an animal, too; to make sex merely another animal appetite. Satan took every opportunity—in Japan and later, too—to get me to consider myself an animal. And he was often successful. When I looked in the mirror and what I saw could not be distinguished as human, when what I saw looked more like a dead dog, run over on the highway, I felt a revulsion that seemed to demand that I deny who I was in the eyes of my Maker and Redeemer.

Brenda never ceased focusing on the image of God in which I was made. Brenda's spiritual eyes were never blinded by appearances. Because Brenda loved me and knew that I was still a man made in the image of God and treated me that way, she, through her redemptive love, convinced me that God's image was there no matter how I appeared to the world. Brenda, as the mediator of grace, played the Christlike role in bringing me back to a full understanding of my own dignity. Yes, in Saint Paul's terms, our roles were reversed: Brenda became Christ and I became His bride. But that's not so strange, because we, as Christians—as the church—whether male or female, all play the feminine role to Christ: we are the ugly bride made beautiful in His embrace. Likewise, in the priesthood of all believers, everyone plays the role of Christ, being a member of His body, when he or she is the channel of God's mercy and grace.

One of the complications that occurs in skin grafting is that when your skin is amputated from your body and replaced elsewhere, it shrinks. During my convalescent leave, the skin over my entire neck area gradually shrunk up so tight that it pulled my chin down to my right shoulder until my head was drawn down at a forty-five-degree angle. My right arm and shoulder were drawn up, and my mouth and lip were pulled way down so that my lower teeth were thrust outside my mouth.

When I returned to the ward, the doctors came in and said, "Dave, you see the problem. We are going to do an incision that will run from one side of your neck to the other. Then we'll lay in a big patch of new skin. It's a major operation because it's a huge incision. But we still don't want to put you under general anesthesia, so we're going to put you on a narcotic that will dull enough of the senses to enable you to do everything we tell you to do." So, on November 20, the neck and shoulder contracture was cut open and a big graft taken from my stomach laid in. Only about 70 percent of the graft took hold, so eleven days later the raw areas were regrafted with skin from my thigh. Then two more grafts were necessary before the problem was under control.

About thirty days after the first big release-of-contracture operation on November 20, the doctors planned to start this procedure over again—this time on my shoulder and upper arm to release the contracture that was pulling my arm and shoulder into a knot: the famous Z operation, as they called it, which derived its name from the shape of the incision. I had seen another fellow who had had a similar operation, and his scar looked grotesque. Without anesthesia, and even with pain-killer, the pain from the first operation had been absolutely immense. So I said, "I don't want that operation. I flat prefer that you do not cut that deep on me. I'll handle it my own way."

I conceived a plan of how to do this and carried it through. Every morning I would get up real early and drag an old Samsonite chair along with me to the shower room. One long steel rod ran down through all the shower stalls with each curtain threaded on to it. I pulled the chair in the stall with me, and turned on the hot water so it splashed right on my shoulder. The water always softened up the skin. I would stand up on that chair, put my hand over the shower curtain rod with the water firing straight at me. Then I kicked out the chair from under me. My body weight would stretch that arm up over my head. I would just hang there because I couldn't let go—my fingers were curled and set because of tendon damage and I couldn't have let go even if I had wanted to. I would scream from the pain, and of course the screaming brought the nurses running. They would dash in there, get the chair under me, and chew me out, up, and down. But the next morning I would be back there hanging from the rod, screaming. That was my way, and it worked. I finally got that skin stretched out and that arm working, and I never had any more surgery on it.

I was given a second convalescent leave from December 23 to January 22. When I returned, the doctors were again concerned about the contracture of my neck and the right corner of my mouth. The surgeries weren't complete until February 13. Finally the doctors were through with their cutting, and by March I was on my way out of the intensive care ward.

Although Brenda had gotten an apartment in San Antonio, she was still doing a lot of driving back and forth between San Antonio and Fort Worth in our '65 Mustang, which was starting to show its age. We didn't have much money. Even the money that was to come to me as a completely disabled Vietnam veteran was delayed because of bureaucratic hangups—chiefly because I had initially been reported dead.

But one day I got a package in the mail: my old sea bag, my old boots, and a few personal belongings (among them my wedding ring) which Lt. Rambo had finally retrieved from my locker. Before he had got to my stuff, however, the guys had picked it over. They got my battery-powered Sony television, the fancy cassette recorder on which I had made tapes for Brenda, and all my decent civilian clothes.

In Vietnam I had been paid with "military payment certificates." These MPCs were used to keep greenbacks from being funneled into communist hands; we redeemed them when we got back to the States. Except for a few purchases like the television and the recorder, I hadn't spent much money. The only commodities on the local market were women and alcohol, and since I used neither, I saved a lot of money. I would roll my money up, put a rubber band around it, and when I got a roll about six inches thick, I'd start another roll. I hid these big wads in the toes of my old boots. I guess Lt. Rambo must have had a laugh when he discovered that the guys had ripped off everything except my old boots. They didn't look worth stealing, but they were the real treasure chest.

Anyway, when Brenda opened up the package and started going through the stuff, I said, "Baby, check the left boot. It should be full of money." It was empty. My heart sank, and I said, "They got everything I had." But soon after a letter came addressed to Mrs. David Roever from Lt. Rambo. It was written when Lt. Rambo himself still thought I had died, and in it he praised me for my courage and moral rectitude; also in the envelope was a cashier's check for every penny of my money. I could kiss that guy for making sure my wife got that money. It was almost enough to pay for a brand new car, so I told Brenda, "Babe, just as soon as I can get out of here for a few days, we're going to buy you a new car." So we traded the old Mustang in on a seafoam green Ford Torino, our first brand-new car.

The homeward stretch of my hospitalization began in March, when I was transferred to the regular burn ward. The medical staff threw me a big party. (I was the only one of the thirteen victims I arrived with to survive.) All the nonelective surgery was over and done with: I had a complete sheath of new skin. (If I wanted to have cosmetic work done later that was my business.)

Soon after I was transferred to the regular burn ward in March, a doctor came in to check me over, including checking my ears. I was sprawled out in the bed watching a little television set on my bedside table. The doctor was studying the damage to my right ear, or the hole in my head where the outer ear had been.

He said, "Dave, be still."

"Why?" I asked.

He had this scope or something in my ear, and he joked, "I'm trying to watch television," insinuating that he could see the TV through my head. He was actually setting me up for the bad news. "Dave," he said, "you will never hear out of this ear again."

I heard that very sentence with my right ear. I jumped up and about knocked that guy over. I have never lost my hearing again in that ear except for short periods when the canals close shut due to infections, to which the injury has left me particularly vulnerable. The restoration of hearing in my right ear is truly a miracle.

It seems a good time to recollect, as well, the miraculous recovery of sight in my right eye, which occurred later, about a year after my release from the hospital. Before I left the hospital, they opened up my newly grafted right eyelid. At the time they only cut a narrow slit in my smooth graft of new skin and the eye stayed narrowly open all the time. It looks much more normal now, but I still have no muscle control in that eyelid. My eye has to roll up under the lid to water itself, which is why I tape the lid closed at night. I was thinking about going back to college, and so I went to a clinic for the required physical. The doctor, a friendly white-haired older fellow, had done the blood, heart, and hearing tests and so forth, and said, "Now, let's check your eyes." I had of course told him about my injury and said that my right eye didn't work well. He covered my right eye with a little black card and asked me to read the chart down at the end of the room. I read the big E and the next row and the next row. "Perfect." Then he moved the card to my left eye in order to check my right eye. And I looked, and I swear to you I saw that chart down there as clear as could be. I read that thing. I couldn't finish the bottom line because my eye was starting to water with tears of joy. I got so excited, I jumped to my feet, hit his machine with my chest, and knocked out a bunch of glass lenses which shattered on the floor. I tried to apologize, all the while checking and rechecking the vision in my right eye. That man shared my excitement. He suddenly knew that I had had an incredible healing.

I'm not one to discount miracles, but in all honesty I

have to confess that a fortunate circumstance figures in this one which complicates judging the degree to which God directly intervened in the processes of nature. Later, an eye doctor told me: "It's no medical miracle that you have the thickness of the scar on your lens: that's normal. But what is unusual is that the scar tissue would clear so completely that you could see through it." Apparently the scar tissue has formed in the shape of a perfect lens. I have perfect vision in that eye, although without the continual clearing function the eyelid is meant to perform, it never stops hurting. Ulcers easily develop on it as well because it doesn't blink. Still, I'm more than grateful.

My year of slow crucifixion required much of me, and I know it was as deeply painful to Brenda in another way, as she watched me suffer and lived with my ups and downs from day to day. I could only have endured that year of suffering through the grace granted to me by God in my family, especially my mother and Brenda. I don't feel it required any special bravery on my part: my choices were limited, theirs were not. Particularly Brenda: my wife could have left and started a new life without me, instead she stayed by me.

The most difficult part of my recovery was still to come, however. The hospital provided an insulated, protected, and hence unreal environment which could not and did not prepare me for my new life as a "freak." Where everyone's a freak, as on the burn ward, no one's a freak. But eventually it came time for me to face the everyday world and every-day people.

14

The moment I stepped out of the hospital into the "real" world my identity became an overwhelming issue. The bad side of my face looked like the ball at the tip of a roll-on deodorant bottle—I mean it was so much smooth skin, featureless, Mr. Marble Head.

The first minute I was off the burn ward, I passed a woman with little twins at her side in the hallway. When the children saw me, they went wild with fear. I couldn't blame them. I was pretty hideous to behold. The left side of my face was real pink because the top layers were burned off, but the basic skin was still there looking as if it were sunburned. But on my right side, the eye was covered, the ear was gone, cartilege stuck out from my nose, and my face was blood red from the new skin laid on it. Half my mouth was sewn together and I talked funny. These two young children looked at me and screamed, "Mommy, what is it? Mommy, what is it?"

There's no person in the word *it.* Their question cut me like a sharp knife, causing me the sharpest pain I had felt since I had looked at the mirror in Japan. I looked at them and said, "*It* is a man, kids," and walked off.

I realized that I had to begin accepting a new identity that incorporated—like taking on a skin graft—my freakish appearance. I have measured the process of this healing through noting what has been the narrowing discrepancy between my inner sense of self and my awareness of how I look to other people. I'm still not completely comfortable with my appearance. I let my kids fight to put on my ear, but, curiously, I still can't bear to let them see me with my eye taped shut.

While still in the hospital when I could finally hold a Bible, my folks brought me a beautiful new red *Thompson Chain Reference Bible*, and my dad said, "This is a good study Bible for you and your ministry."

Not long before the presentation of the Bible I had been complaining to Dad about not being out of the hospital yet to get my ministry going. "I want to preach," I said with emphatic resentment. "Doctors doctor, nurses nurse, and preachers preach."

He said, "Well, have you prepared a message?"

"Why should I prepare a message if there's no place to preach?" I asked.

And he replied quietly, "And why give you a place to preach if you don't have a message?" Gently but shrewdly, he nipped my self-pity right in the bud. He treated me like a man with a vocation, a responsibility, and that helped give me the confidence to believe I had a vocation. So I wrote two sermons.

After they had been written, in walked one of my faithful visitors, a pastor named James Brothers, with an invitation to preach twice at his church in a few weeks. Of course I accepted, not letting on that I wasn't yet permitted to leave the hospital. I would have to sneak out.

"When do you want me to come pick you up?" he asked.

I said, "Sunday morning, real early."

I worked on my messages, and when the morning came, I had to crawl underneath the nurses' station wearing only my hospital robe. I took my old blue jeans and my pajama top, the only clothes I had. The only thing I had for my feet were the flimsy little slip-on floppers we wore in the hospital. I met him out in the parking lot after pulling on my jeans in the dark behind a tree. There I was, in jeans, pajamas, robe, and slippers, with one eye and one ear. And my skin was at stake, literally. At that point my skin was so fresh and delicate you could push on it with your finger and it would come right off.

Pastor Brothers, thinking I had permission to leave the hospital, said, "Now, I want you to spend the whole day with us." I was relieved because that meant I didn't have to sneak out twice.

I will never forget that morning at his church. We got there early, and I sat in the front pew with my back to the congregation and my left arm up on the back of the pew. Only my left profile was visible—it was red, but not distorted. When Pastor Brothers invited me up to speak, and I got up to walk to the pulpit, the people suddenly realized I was wearing a hospital robe, not a coat. I walked to the pulpit, turned around, laid my Bible down, and faced the congregation. I shocked those poor folks near to death. Women put their handkerchiefs to their mouths and ran for the ladies' room. I stood up there thinking to myself—just like the scene with the little twins—*God, why did I do this? Look what I did to them.* It was like I could hear voices whispering in my ear: *You monster. You know you are a monster. You creep. Look what you are doing to these people. You are a freak. It will always be this way. You've missed your calling, buddy. You belong in a circus side-show.*

Yes, the Devil stood close by, but the Word of God in my heart began to minister to me: "Faithful is he that calleth you, who also will do it." And I put the whole thing in my Father's hands. I started to preach. I didn't tell the people that morning about Vietnam. All I did was preach Christ crucified. When I got through preaching my message, I gave an invitation. Broad-shouldered, hairy-chested men walked down that aisle, tears streaming down their faces, and gave their hearts to Christ. I knew my ministry had begun.

I spent the afternoon at Rev. Brothers's house. His little kids were scared to death of me, so he took them to someone else's house for the day. I remember watching an NFL play-off game on the television and thinking that maybe I could lead a normal life after all.

That evening, when I preached again, I spoke for the first time about Vietnam and my recuperation. People cried all the way through it, more out of pity than anything else. That was fine for then, but I began to understand that if I told the story again I would have to diffuse the pity somehow, perhaps through humor, in order for the message in the story to strike home.

This book is the most detailed and straightforward rendering of the experience I have ever attempted. I can let the events of the story speak for themselves here, in a way that is impossible when I am speaking face to face in front of an audience. Now more than ever I do not want anyone's pity. I want to testify that the kingdom and the power and the glory all belong to Christ Jesus.

Two weeks before being officially discharged from Brooke, I was placed in an out-patient clinic where I met a kid, John, who had had his leg amputated after a motorcycle accident. Two city buses had collided head-on, with him in between. It was incredible that he lived. He had been in the army only one day when it happened. He had been sworn in—he had never even put the uniform on—but he was still entitled to veteran benefits.

Since I was about to be discharged, Brenda had gone back with her folks to Fort Worth, and I had our car to use. I had begun driving out every night to a church youth camp in Kerrville, Texas, run by Laurell Akers, about seventy miles away. One day this young amputee asked me where I went every night. The kid had a foul mouth; this and other signs showed his need of Christ. So I said, "I go out with a whole bunch of young people, friends of mine." I wasn't going to say I was going to a party. I didn't want to lie to him. I could have just said "youth camp," but that wouldn't have made any sense without further explanation. John was into smoking pot in a big way, and figured I was going to a pot party. He probably thought I was hemming and hawing because I was afraid to come right out and say I was doing drugs.

Young John got excited. "I want to go with you."

I said, "All right." So we took off.

As we left San Antonio on I-10 toward Kerrville, John said, "Now where was it you said we were going?"

I said, "We are going to a church youth camp." That guy grabbed the door handle like he would have jumped out of the car if I hadn't been doing the speed limit on the interstate. Not a good idea, as I knew from my childhood experience. I said, "John, you asked to go and we are going."

When we got there he saw all of the girls, so he decided maybe he could stay through supper. Then we started over toward the old outdoor tabernacle where they had the chapel services and he could hear the organ, the guitars, and the drums jamming, warming up.

"Wow, man," John said, "we *are* going to have a party, aren't we?"

"Could be, John," I said, "could be. You may even meet some important people tonight." Of course I was hoping that one of them was going to be Jesus.

That night a young preacher got up and preached a fantastic message. When he got through with his message, he gave an invitation. John looked over at me and he trembled. With tears in his eyes, he asked me, "What are you going to do?"

"It's not what I'm going to do that matters, John. What are you going to do?"

I will never forget his answer. He pointed at his head and said, "Up here these people are fools." Then he pointed at his heart and said, "Down here I want to be one of them so bad."

"Which are you going to listen to, your head or your heart?"

He sat there a minute. Then he said slowly, "Well, I think I will be one of them."

Now he had on his artificial leg and little aluminum crutches that wrap around the arm. He clamored to his feet, and we started down the aisle together. The kids turned around and looked at us. Here comes a cripple escorted by a monster. I still had only one eye and one ear and the right side of my head was feature-less, just smooth skin. Here come two guys really hurting in their lives. One of them is leading his buddy to Christ. It was beautiful. When Laurell Akers explained something of what had happened the kids just melted in their seats.

The first words John said when he got up from his knees were, "I've got to get back to the hospital because I've got some friends who need to know about this."

Something happened to me that evening, too: this was another event which helped to confirm my call to be an evangelist. I too could hardly wait to get back to the hospital . . . and get out of there to begin my work.

*A*fter spending the summer at a VA hospital in Dallas, closer to home, I was discharged from the hospital in September of 1970. Through that fall and winter, despite my conviction about my calling, I was in the throes of putting together a new Dave Roever, getting used to a new way of appearing to the world and to myself, trying to find my place as a freak.

I had no problem accepting Brenda's love when she kissed me and said, "Welcome home, Davey," and months later when we were able to be more intimate. But I'm no saint. Learning to accept unconditional love, Brenda's or Christ's, has been for me no simple lesson learned once and for all. After I got out of the hospital and had to begin facing life in the real world, I gave Brenda problems.

I played with her the same game most of us play with Christ: I couldn't accept her love for me until I thought I was acceptable. I even resented her love for me, because I hadn't earned it; I didn't deserve it. Her love for me was an insult to my pride, and it gave me no room for selfish self-pity. Christ accepted me and Brenda accepted me, but Dave Roever often had difficulty accepting himself. He was too ugly. What he saw in the mirror wasn't what he wanted to see. To admit that others could love me in my disfigured state meant my disfigurement was real—once I let myself see it and accept it through Brenda's eyes, I could no longer pretend I didn't look the way I did. My pride dictated that I keep up the pretension of my own inviolability despite the massive evidence to the contrary: that's how strong pride, original sin, can be; that's also how pretentious, for it would have us act as if we were our own gods. One of my friends once told me that, in the Fall, mankind did not lose the ability to love as much as the ability to feel or accept being loved. I can testify to that.

I have to make a painful confession here. There was a selfish malice in my heart at that time that made my face look beautiful in comparison. Do you know what I would say to Brenda if I wanted something and I didn't get it? If, for instance, I wanted to be intimate and she didn't, or if I wanted to buy a new car or camper, and she didn't, or if I wanted a certain meal and she didn't want to fix it? I would say to her, "Well, I don't blame you; I couldn't love me either." After her faithfulness to me, that was a rotten thing to say. And, Lord have mercy, He knows I must have said it a dozen times.

That woman never said a word. Never.

And every time I said it, I knew I was stabbing her in the heart.

For a while she was thinking of taking a job to earn some extra income—we were saving toward buying a house. The thought of her working was tremendously threatening to me; if she went out into the world to work, she would be confronted daily with men far more attractive than I. One day we quarreled about it, and then I accused her again: "I don't blame you; I couldn't love me either."

She said nothing. I blew up. I went over, grabbed my coat, put it on in a big huff, and stormed out of the house. When I slammed the door, I caught my coat, and I had to open the door and get my coat out, which really frosted me. I slammed the door again, which made a big racket like slamming shut a bread box because we were living in a little travel-trailer at the time. I had a Ford pickup as a second vehicle, and I put that old truck in reverse, slammed the pedal to the floor, and skidded backward out into the street. I slid to a stop, pulled it into gear, spun the tires, and took off down the road.

A half-mile down the highway I glanced out the rearview mirror and what did I see but our Torino right behind me. Brenda was chasing me down that road. The new car had no trouble keeping up with the truck, which I found positively maddening. I was angered anyway that she had followed me, so I slid over onto the shoulder of the highway, gravel pinging the hub caps and dust blowing up under that old pickup, and I skidded to a stop. I looked back. She had stopped right behind me. I got out, slammed the truck door shut, and walked back to the car.

She rolled down the window and looked up at me sheepishly.

I looked at her and said, "Where do you think you're going?"

She looked back at me, shrugged her shoulders, and said, "I don't know. Where are you going? I always went with you." There were tears in her eyes, her cheeks and neck were mottled, red and white, from the heat of her emotion.

I looked at her and what I said is the most horrible statement I have ever made in my life. I looked at her and said, "Well, I don't know where I'm going either, but I'm going anywhere to get away from you."

And then she said, "What did I ever do to you to make you want to get away from me?"

"Brenda," I said, "every time I say, 'I don't blame you; I couldn't love me either,' you don't answer. You just stand there. Well, I guess I know why you don't say anything— because you can't love me. Now you're going out to get a job and find someone else and I don't blame you. So see, you don't love me. Who could?"

She opened the door of that car, got out, and stood up on her tiptoes so we were nose to nose. She looked me in the eye and said, "You want me to say something? You want me to tell you why I never said anything? Because the ignorance of such a statement didn't deserve the honor of an intelligent reply."

That's all she said.

I threw my arms around her. I was a little boy. I was just a little boy, trying to say, "Mommy, mommy, I've got an owie. Kiss my owie." I was a little boy in the arms of a giant of a woman. I wanted to curl up in her lap and let her hold me. I said to her, when I could talk, "Brenda, as long as I live, I swear to you before heaven this day, I will never use those words against you again." And I haven't.

That day I let myself be loved, which meant that I let myself be Dave Roever, the wounded soldier, the burn victim, the disfigured beast. But if my beauty could truly love this beast, then he was no mere beast but someone made in the image of God, despite outward appearances. If she could truly love this incarnation of me, then I could try to love the new me. I could at least start trying to accept the change.

Eventually through Brenda's continued care, I lost the fear which haunted my dreams, a powerful fear involved in the argument that day—my terror that she would leave me. In my own heart I didn't know if I had it within *me* to love a spouse such as I was, but apparently she did. She *didn't want* an "out." She *wanted* me, her husband, for better and for worse. That's love.

Laurell L. Akers,
Pastor,
Glad Tidings
Assembly of God
Houston, Texas.

Brenda, Kimberly (9), Dave, Matthew (11).

Below: Back in Vietnam as an evangelist, Dave is with a Vietnamese pastor and an American missionary at a church in Vung Tau.

Dave speaks to students at a school assembly in Dayton, Ohio.

Above: (Left) The Southern California Billy Graham Crusade, Anaheim Stadium, July 20, 1985. (Right) Dave speaking to an audience of 65,000 in Anaheim Stadium. Below: Dave with a Vietnam veteran who responded at the Graham crusade in Anaheim.

These R-COM (Roever Communications) trucks house state-of-the-art equipment used to produce "The Dave Roever Crusade," a weekly television program aired on the Trinity Broadcasting Network.

Above: Standing room only for the first Dave Roever city-wide crusade—August, 1986, Lufkin, Texas. Below: Dave and his family spend most of the year traveling throughout the country in their bus home.

From left: Jack Cousins, a Billy Graham team member; Dave; and Tom Westhall, chaplain at Andrews Air Force Base in Washington, D. C.

Below: The Roever family at Anaheim in 1985. From left: Matthew (14), Dave, Brenda, and Kimberly (12).

16

*B*y winter, we had a fourteen-foot-wide house trailer—we had really moved up in the world; now we had a camper and a house trailer, neither one paid for. We had been there in Fort Worth for about four months, and we were living on my social security and VA pension—medical retirement, it's called. Between the two checks I could have lived the rest of my life with my feet propped up watching soaps and football on television.

I was sitting in the trailer one day in January, 1971, when we heard a knock at the door. I looked outside, and I couldn't believe it. Standing on the doorstep was Laurell Akers, all the way from Houston. Laurell had been an important part of my teen years: from the time I was twelve and continuing for six years, this man had included me in every summer youth camp program he had conducted in South Texas. Not only that, but he had taken me on vacations after each camp program and had made it possible for me to meet and associate with the major church leaders in the state. It was so good to see him. With tears of joy, I threw my arms around my old friend and led him into the house. He agreed to stay for dinner, so we sat and talked while Brenda cooked a real fine chicken-fried steak dinner.

After dinner we retired to the living room. "Laurell, what brings you to Fort Worth?" I asked.

"Well, it's kind of strange, Dave," he said and looked away. He was stuttering and stammering and finally he just looked me right in the eye and said, "I'm not getting off this couch, I'm not walking out that door, I'm not leaving here until you promise me you will be the associate minister at my church." This was his way of saying, *Dave, I love you, and I've got confidence in you. Nothing is going to change your dreams or keep them from coming to pass.*

I looked at him and said, "What? What did you say?"

"I'm not getting off this couch, walking out that door, or leaving this house until you have promised me that you will be my associate pastor."

"Well, Laurell, just move on in because I am not going to be any pastor." I couldn't see myself being able to fill that role. All I could see was a roll-on Cyclops making people gag.

We talked some more. I asked, "What could I do?"

"I need somebody who will help understand the hurting people of my church. I need somebody to minister to the people who suffer, somebody they can trust. You're the man." And he reached out his hands toward me. I thought to myself, *Dear God, he wants me. Somebody wants me.* I went wild. I was saying, *No, no, no,* and all the time I was thinking, *Yes, yes, yes.* I let him beg me awhile. That appealed to my pride. I didn't want him to imagine that I was thinking, *Oh, Laurell, you're my last hope.* But that was close to the truth.

I looked at him and said, "Well, let me pray about it."

He said, "Let's pray right now." He wasn't going to let anything ride.

I said to Brenda, "Baby, what do you think about it?"

"Davey, it's a chance to get started." There's something about the way she says "Davey" to me: I swear, I would attempt anything if she said, "Davey, try it."

"Okay, Laurell, the answer is yes."

He shouted "Hallelujah," clapped his hands, and said, "let's make some plans." We started planning.

We talked late into the night. Laurell slept over with us and returned the next morning to Houston. I couldn't sleep that night I was so excited and happy. Within a couple weeks we sold our house trailer and headed for Houston in our little travel trailer.

We got the trailer set up in the parking lot, and were welcomed with real thanksgiving by the church. I began preaching on Wednesday nights.

I received no pay for being assistant pastor, incidentally. Glad Tidings Assembly of God was a little bitty church. But letting me preach was pay enough. Oh man, I felt like King Kong in a fur coat up in that pulpit. I would put my tie on, and go to it. And the dignity, which Brenda had always seen implanted in my soul, became something I could feel once again.

Real soon I said to myself, *There's no way I'm going to live off the government dole when I can work at my calling.* So one day I picked up the phone and called social security and said, "If you don't mind, would ya'll not mail any more checks to me? Take me off the computer. I feel like I'm bumming off my country."

The woman on the phone said, "Who is this?" I gave her my name and number again and she looked it up and said, "Sir, this is disability pay. You've earned this. You've paid your money in. It's yours."

I said, "It's not really mine because I'm not disabled."

"Oh. You're all better?"

"Yes ma'am, I'm doing real good now." Here I was with one eye, one ear, one thumb, and one good preaching finger, but I finally convinced her.

She told me it all had to be in writing and I would have to do this and that. I did it, and the next month there was no check in the mail.

Then I had to get a money-paying job or we wouldn't be able to keep food on the table. So I went down and found a job at the Concrete Coring Company in the office where my brother worked. He pulled some strings for me; he was such a good employee, they were willing to take his say-so about my abilities.

I had never been an office manager before, didn't know diddly-squat, but I learned quickly, and good money started coming in.

We needed it because in March of 1971 our son Matthew was born. Given the high incidence of sterility among burn victims, Matthew was a great sign to us of God's blessing. It was a way of God telling us that life was going to go on, that my injury would hamper us less and less in the future, that our endeavors would prove fruitful. But Matthew's birth was more than a symbol; I got a great kick out of being a daddy. I remember looking at his fingernails as an infant: they were just like mine, so small and yet perfect duplicates. (Nearly a fully grown man now, he strongly favors me, and, while it's not always good to live through your children, God willing, it will be fun to see how my looks might have developed through my twenties and further on thereafter.)

Preacher after preacher after preacher in the area had begun calling up and asking, "Would you come to speak at our church on Sunday night and share your story with us?" Laurell let me go out on Sunday night so that I could accept these invitations. I was making big dollars during the week, and people were giving me money to share my story on the weekends.

One day Laurell looked at me and said, "You know you are not being a very good assistant pastor when you are gone all the time."

"And you know," I said, "you intended for this to happen." He smiled big.

Brenda and I had also begun traveling as evangelists on short trips with a woman named Karen Crews. She had a choir of about fifty kids who sang in sign language, the Signs for the Harvest Singers. Many of Karen's family were deaf, and she had finally gone into full-time ministry to the deaf after being an English teacher at the school I had attended as a kid. She was doing well in her evangelistic work, people loved the Harvest Singers, but she did need an evangelist. So she asked me if I would travel full-time with the choir. The pay was modest at best, but I enjoyed working with Karen, and I was able to always keep my family with me—a matter of top priority in my life that continues today. We ate in the homes of the people, but I pulled our little travel-trailer so that Brenda, Matthew, and I could have a private family life together. Our work with Karen took more and more time, but we would come back through and stop in at Laurell's as often as we could. We parked at his house when we had a few days. I was still preaching for him occasionally.

One morning, Laurell and I were sitting at his kitchen table, drinking coffee and talking together as we did every day when I was in town. This was in 1972, and the Vietnam War was still going, but everyone could see the end coming. The troops were going to be pulled out before much longer. Laurell suddenly stopped, put his cup down, looked across the table at me, and said, "You know, Dave, when Vietnam is over, your ministry will be over."

That statement hit me like a baseball bat across the bridge of my nose. He implied that my testimony would be interesting only as long as Vietnam was on the news. He implied that my identity, my calling, depended on circumstances. I thought he was implying that I didn't have much to say except for a sympathy-raising, blood-and-guts testimony of wartime faith and courage. I thought he was prophesying the eventual failure of my ministry, my vocation; that he believed my identity as an evangelist was fraudulent.

I looked at him and everything in me hated him. I hated my best friend. "When Vietnam is over, your ministry will be over." After all I had worked through, was that to be the epitaph on my service to the Lord?

I slid my coffee cup away, leaned back in my chair at a

forty-five-degree angle, and shot him my most severe look of disgust, never saying a word. Then I got up, walked out his door, and slammed it shut behind me. (I was good at slamming doors.) I opened the trailer door and yelled in to Brenda, "Baby, we're leaving."

She said, "Oh, we got another meeting?"

I said, "We've got bunches of meetings. We're not coming back here. We will never darken his door again."

"Good grief," she said, "what happened?"

"He just told me that when Vietnam is over, my ministry will be over."

Brenda didn't say anything. She just sat there thinking. I backed the car around, hitched up the trailer, and we hit the road.

For a year, Brenda and I traveled full-time with Karen Crews and her choir, and I made numerous contacts. It seemed as if every place we went, the pastor said, "Will you come back and hold us a meeting? We would like you to stay a week or two or three." We began booking dates on our own, and before long I had a solid year of speaking engagements ahead of me, mostly invitations to small churches. So within three years after I got out of the hospital, Brenda and I had made an encouraging start in our evangelistic work. And our family was growing; in June of 1973 my joy in life was multiplied beyond my wildest expectations with the birth of our daughter Kimberly—our beautiful little girl.

The same summer Kimberly was born, Brenda and I went to what was called an indoor camp meeting at the Will Rogers Coliseum in Forth Worth to hear Bernard Johnson, a famous evangelist from Brazil. (Today he draws crowds of a hundred thousand people there.) As Rev. Johnson told of the great work God was doing overseas, I heard, "overseas, overseas," but I began thinking, *Vietnam, Vietnam.*

As we left the meeting that night, I felt strongly that God was calling me to go back to Vietnam as a missionary evangelist: to go back, as I began saying, not with an M–16 but with John 3:16. On the way home we stopped at a red light on Seventh Street. While we waited for the light to change, I looked right at Brenda and said, "Sweetheart, I believe God spoke to me tonight."

She looked right back at me and said, "You're going back to Vietnam, aren't you?" She had received the same word from the Lord. "How are we going to pay for it?" she asked.

I said, "Sweetheart, if God is in it, the money will be there. I'm not worried about that."

As if to confirm the Lord's leading, once I'd made the commitment to go to Vietnam, we began to see an increase in the offerings and honorariums we received. I remember mentioning my dream in a message at a church in Crockett, Texas, hoping someone would catch my vision. Afterwards, a little old lady came up to me and said, "My husband died and left a large amount of insurance money. I'm trying to find ministries to put it in, and I feel led to underwrite your trip to Vietnam."

Now, *this* preacher's kid, Dave Roever, gives money to widows; I don't take money from widows. I said, "Dear lady, thank you for your love and your commitment to our ministry, but I have to say, 'No ma'am.'" She began to insist, but it was as though the Lord were standing behind her, shaking His head, saying, *No, you don't do it.*

I said, explaining, "Ma'am, I can't do it. God doesn't want one person to be the sole supporter. He wants it to be a number of people who will receive a reward for their investment in souls. You can make a modest contribution if you like, but I will not permit you or anyone to foot the whole bill." She kept insisting—God bless her heart—but I finally talked her out of it.

The pastor had been standing nearby, and when we got out to the car, he said, "Roever, you're incredible. I've had four evangelists in this church who came here for the purpose of talking her out of her money for their big-time ministries. Now when she is finally ready to give it to somebody, he won't take it. That is about the most amazing thing I've ever seen."

I believe more today than ever that the Lord was testing me to see if I would trust Him to sponsor that trip. In the end, the trip cost ten thousand dollars. That included travel expenses as well as living expenses for three months in Vietnam. The money came in, so I went in January of 1974, after getting a visa—despite having been told by nearly everyone that obtaining one was out of the question. The war was still going on, but the U.S. troops had been pulled out. In one sense it was not easy to go—it was not easy for me to leave my family. This would be my first extended separation from them, but it was something I knew I must do.

I stopped in Japan on my way with the express purpose of visiting Paul Klahr, the missionary who had spent three days of his family time tracking down a kid he had never seen nor heard of. When Paul met me at the airport, he asked me why I'd come. I said, "Paul, I came for one reason: to say 'thank you' for coming to me in my hour of need." God blessed me for doing that. I felt as the leper must have who went back to thank Jesus. I ended up staying in Japan for a couple of weeks, helping Paul with some evangelistic meetings.

When I got to Vietnam, I met Irving Rutherford and Aaron Rothganger, two wonderful men who worked with Teen Challenge to help solve the drug addiction problem among both the military and civilian population. Because of my military experience there, I was able to establish good contacts with some of the high-level officers in the Vietnamese army. For the first time the Vietnamese military was admitting that drug abuse was not just an American problem.

They had gotten as far as transforming the Long Ben jail into a detoxification center, but their "detox program" wasn't very sophisticated; it wasn't humane, for that matter, or effective. They tossed addicts in, locked them up, and made them go cold turkey. Then the addicts were turned loose, and of course, in ten minutes they were back on drugs.

We went into the former jail and saw addicts from seven to seventy years old. Women were living right there with the men. It was a swine pit, a good image for the place the Prodigal Son landed. I didn't see a nurse in the place, no doctors, no methadone, no nothing. No one had his own individual cell. They threw these people in the middle of the facility and gave them food, as if they were animals. I'm sure the death rate was higher than the detox rate.

For several years, Teen Challenge had been trying to build a detoxification center in Saigon. When I got there, they had just appropriated property in a vacant park and were clearing it. I helped out, mostly by warning them against tossing old explosive devices and ammunition that still might be live into one pile, as they had been doing.

I made contacts with pastors through Aaron Rothganger and started preaching in the cities that weren't yet in communist hands. We drew big crowds. We went out along what was called the "highway of death" between Saigon and Vungtau to a big refugee settlement run by the Assemblies of God, who had done more than just send in preachers. They had gone in and built hundreds of little houses out of wood—with concrete foundations and toilets and a sewer system. Those refugees lived in splendor compared to the usual hooches the people patched together, which always reeked of human feces and the smell of death. I was proud of what these missionaries had done.

They welcomed me and were glad I had come to preach to the refugees. We had three services, averaging three thousand Vietnamese each day. The response was absolutely dynamite. The only disappointment of the entire occasion was the loneliness that came from not having my family with me. We are, and always have been, close-knit, and I missed them terribly.

When the money ran out, I came home and immediately

began making plans to return. In January of 1975, I went back to Asia, this time taking my wife and kids with me as far as Japan. For three months, using Japan as my home base, I made trips in and out of Vietnam to continue my evangelistic efforts there. I did virtually the same thing on these trips as I had done on the first one. By then, however, the communists had taken over more cities, and it was clear that the South Vietnamese were losing the war.

I went to Da Nang, which was thoroughly infiltrated with communists. In one old bombed-out school gymnasium, we held a service attended by 573 Vietnamese Buddhist students. They asked me right out loud, in Vietnamese of course, "What happened to you, sir?" At that time my face was still red and angry looking. And these folks, like everyone else, were taken aback by my appearance. So I stood there and shared my testimony. I could still speak some Vietnamese, but I wasn't good at religious terms. In Vietnamese I knew how to speak the language of the war but not of the gospel. I counted on Major Lem of the ARVN (one of several committed Christians in the top ranks of the military) as my interpreter.

I told them that I had come originally as a soldier to their country because I believed that they had the inherent right to be free, just as the Americans, the French, or the Japanese do. "But freedom never comes without a price," I said; and I explained that I'd been severely injured when a grenade blew up in my face while I was fighting for their freedom.

The Vietnamese are very tender-hearted people. These young men sat there with tears dripping from their chins and I really felt the Lord was touching their hearts. Then I said, "But I want to tell you about another man who fought for your freedom because He cares so much about you. His name is Jesus Christ. He's not one who lets your good health depend on luck. He's not going to let your tomorrows depend on chance. God has a will for your life. This Jesus fought for your freedom. He was murdered when He was in

His thirties because His life was a threat to those who didn't believe Him when He said He was the Son of God. They killed Him. He died to liberate Vietnamese students just as much as He died for Dave Roever; He died to liberate the whole world from the captivity of our sins. And I'm going to tell you something. He's even here tonight. Right now, Jesus is in this place."

These guys leaped to their feet and were looking around for Him.

"No, no," I said, "not where you can see Him with your eyes, but He's here in spirit. You cannot see a spirit, but the Spirit of Jesus Christ is in this place." Then I explained how Jesus could be both with the Father and with us, that we are the body of Christ and whenever we gathered in His name, His spirit is with us. Those young men could not have been more attentive.

Then at the end of my message I said, "I'm going to invite you to accept Jesus. To show that you are really ready to invite Jesus into your heart and life, I want you to stand on your feet, come forward to the front of this building, and let that be a symbolic statement that you are willing to leave your old Buddhist traditions, your godless religion of good luck, and you're willing to say 'Jesus Christ, I believe You are the Son of God and I commit my life to You.'" When I gave the invitation, the entire audience came forward! I was dumbfounded.

I said, "Go back and sit down." So they sat down. I said, "You don't understand. Make sure you understand. No rice is going to be given to you. No new home will be given to you (although, as it turned out, these people would be given new homes through the Assemblies of God building program). No money will be given to you. This is not a ticket to America. I am only saying that you will be forgiven of your sins, your evil deeds, and you will be changed in a way that will make you want to forsake your old ways and accept the new ways of Jesus Christ. You will be given a Bible and you should study it.

"Now, all of you who understand and still want to make this commitment, come forward."

All 573 got up and came forward.

So, for the third time, instead of making them sit down, I said, "I've got to make sure your understand what you are doing." And I went through the whole thing again. They got to chuckling at me because they thought that I thought they didn't know what they were doing. Well, they finally convinced me. And that night, when I led them in their sinners' prayer, when they took the first baby steps of faith, I saw tears in their eyes. They made their confession of sin to Christ and genuinely accepted Him as their Lord.

I was in Saigon in March when the government collapsed and the communists were about to capture the capital city. I knew it was time to leave when half of my hotel was blown up. I was sitting in my room, documenting my trip on a small recorder when all of a sudden I heard a whoosh outside my window, followed by a wham. Then machine-gun fire broke out around the foot of the hotel. (You can hear the bomb and the rat-a-tat-tat on the tape I have.)

I pulled back the curtain and peeked out the window. The whole wing of the hotel opposite the lobby had collapsed. I saw tracers everywhere. I said, "Oh Jesus, help me." It shook me good. My first thought was to get to the Vietnamese people who loved me and would hide me. I knew that if I were captured, I would be treated as a POW, not as some tourist. But then a helicopter team came in and fought back, and by the next morning, the fighting had cleared away.

In the morning I called Irving Rutherford of Teen Challenge—the phones were still working, surprisingly—and said, "Irving, I think you and I need to get out of here."

He said, "Dave, I can't go. I don't care if the communists take it. I've got a job to do here."

"Irving, you've got to get out. You won't have a job to do here when they take it."

He said, "Well, I'm going to take my chances."

I said, "Irving, I can't afford to stay. I have a history that these people would love to pry out of my head. I'm taking the next flight out." (Eventually Irving did get out, and he has since established a new and thriving Teen Challenge Center in Djakarta, Indonesia.)

I couldn't get through on the phone to the airport, so I simply went there. The place was mobbed with people trying to get tickets and fly out. I had a ticket already, but not for that day. I walked up to the gate, and the official never looked at the date of my ticket, the flight number, or anything. Anyone who had a ticket could get on, and I did. It was open seating. People were scrambling for seats, trying to carry chickens—all sorts of stuff—onto this airplane. That Air France 747 was the only commercial plane on the runway, and the news from then on was that the airport had been closed. To my knowledge, I got the last flight out.

From Saigon I flew to Thailand where I stayed to hold some evangelistic meetings before returning home. These meetings were on the busiest street in Bangkok where I opened a coffee shop and gave free donuts to the GIs who walked the streets looking for drugs and women. Many young men and their hookers gave their lives to Christ.

A month or so after I was back in the States, I was holding a meeting in Lufkin, Texas. One night after the service, the pastor and I hung around talking. I needed to get to bed, yet something kept me there, just talking. When the phone rang in the church office, Rev. Freeze said, "Probably a wrong number. Nobody could be calling the church at this hour of the night." But it kept ringing, and he finally said, "Well, I'd better answer it. Maybe it's urgent." He fumbled for his keys, dropped them, and then finally got the office unlocked. The phone was still ringing. He answered, and it turned out to be a person-to-person call for me from Aaron Rothganger.

Aaron said, "Dave, I've just returned home and I'm

calling from Springfield, Missouri. I thought you would want to know: Seventy of those 573 people who accepted Christ that night in Da Nang have been executed because of their faith. They're your babies." That's the way he put it: "They're your babies."

I slammed the phone down. I was so mad at God I almost wanted to curse Him. I stormed out right past Rev. Freeze and said, "I'll see you tomorrow." He didn't have any idea what was going on.

Our little travel-trailer was parked beside the church. It was late, and Brenda and the kids were already in bed. I slammed the door—not caring who I woke up—and walked over to the full-length mirror. I grabbed my shirt and ripped it right off. Buttons popped everywhere, some ricocheting off the ceiling. I couldn't get that shirt off fast enough. I stripped myself to the waist and exposed all my grotesque scars and stood there yelling at the mirror: "Now, God, tell me it was worth it. If something good would have come out of it, then maybe. But this is just Tu Tua all over again. How could you have let this happen?"

I was so mad I went over and fell on the bed, bouncing Brenda halfway off the other side. I put my face in the pillow and screamed at God, "You're not fair. You're not fair. You're not fair." My chest vibrated from these half-growling screams that came right from the soul.

God began to soothe me. It had to be His Spirit that touched my heart. The Lord said to me, *Where do you think those seventy are?*

I lay there exhausted, and said, *Well, I guess they're in heaven.*

He said, *Where do you think they wanted to be?*

I remembered the little hooches where they had lived as refugees in squalid poverty. They lived with disease and malnutrition. They lived with the sound of rocket and gun and mortar fire, in the devastation of fire, with the scars of fire. I said, *God, they are where they have been wanting to go all along. I'm the one still stuck here.* The verse that kept me

alive in my moment of death came back to me as I prayed
for these new martyrs of the faith: "To live is Christ, and to
die is gain."

In the five years since I had stormed out of Laurell
Akers's kitchen to start my own ministry, I had been all
over the country, all over the southwestern United
States—Louisiana, Mississippi, Arkansas, New Mexico,
Texas—I had been to Vietnam as an evangelist and had
preached in Japan and Thailand. Our ministry had become
totally self-sufficient; financially, we were completely on
our own. The Vietnam War was over and my ministry was
growing by leaps and bounds.

I had returned to Vietnam to bring a message of healing,
to minister to the wounds of war and drug addiction, and
while there I began to realize that American GIs, veterans,
and American students needed the same message as Buddhist students and ARVN vets. I was one of how many thousands who had gone over. Now I was one of how many
thousands who had returned wounded, scarred in body
and soul. Just as I had felt responsible that early morning in
college as I listened to the news of the war on the radio—
responsible for those who were fighting the communists in
Vietnam—so I began to realize my responsibility for those
Vietnam vets who were fighting dejection, lost ideals, drug
addiction, joblessness, resentment, and rejection at the
hands of wives, friends, and country. I was scarred in body
but beginning to feel almost whole in spirit. Why? Because I
had come home to a "Welcome home, Davey; I love you,"
from the lips of a wife who had remained faithful. I had
received the same message from my family, my church, and
my Lord. I had begun to realize that what Brenda had given
me, I, in turn, needed to give to my comrades who had
returned without hearing, "Welcome home."

I had a lot of buddies out there who had suffered third-
degree burns of the soul from infidelity and inhumanity,

who had returned vulnerable to the terrorist tactics of an America which had happily accepted the very assumptions of the enemy: that man is an animal, satisfied by the pleasures of this world and the lust of the flesh, if he can procure them.

In every meeting where I preached from 1975 until today, I ask the Vietnam vets to rise, and I ask the congregation to repeat after me, "Welcome home." And I bring my fellows-in-arms the message that Jesus wants to welcome them to His home, where there are many mansions.

The ministry we have today, in large measure, really began, not ended, with the withdrawal of our troops from Vietnam. (Today our ministry also includes the counseling work of Mickey Block—one of my former team mates in Vietnam—who, in his travels under the aegis of our ministry, counsels with Vietnam vets free of charge in every city where he speaks.)

As this all got started I took pride in having proved Laurell Akers wrong.

One day as Brenda and the kids and I were driving through Houston, pulling our Airstream camper behind us, I looked over and saw a phone booth. It had to have been the Lord who put these words in my mind: *Stop and call Laurell Akers.*

When I believe God says something to me, I try not to argue. I swerved onto that exit ramp off Interstate 45 and stopped in front of the phone booth. "What are you doing?" Brenda asked.

I said, "I'm going to call Laurell."

"You're kidding."

I put in the dime and dialed his number. He answered, and I said just one word, "Laurell."

Without a moment's hesitation, he replied, "Dave, I thought you'd never call." It was as though he had been sitting by that phone for five years. He said, "Where are you?" I told him, and he said, "Come on over right away."

I hung up and got back in the car. I don't think the whole

conversation took more than a minute. Brenda asked where we were going. I said, "To Laurell's." She didn't say a word in reply.

I pulled up the long lane in front of his little church. He was living in a house-trailer, and I walked up to the door. It was still open as if I had just walked out. When he heard me at the door, he hollered, "Come in," and I did. Ten feet from the door was the kitchen table, one chair tipped back against the wall at a forty-five-degree angle, half a cup of coffee on the table in front of it, and Laurell sitting on the other side looking at me.

I wasn't going to spoil what I knew he had done. I sat down and just started sipping my coffee, not a word. He said, "Well, what do you think? The war ending going to finish you?"

"You made me mad," I said. "Five years ago you threatened me, you questioned the one scrap of identity I had. While you were at it, you jeopardized the deepest friendship I've ever known. I walked out of this place, opened my Bible, and I built my ministry on the Bible to prove to you— the man who put the challenge before me—that I could found my ministry on the Word of God, not on a mere testimony about Vietnam. And I did. I beat you, Laurell."

He said quietly, "You beat me, Dave."

And I knew then that he had said what he said five years before only to make me respond as I had. He knew that he alone was in the position to push this fledgling out of the nest so that I could fly. Laurell had won. And the Lord Jesus had been glorified. "Laurell," I said, "Laurell . . ." and my emotions started to take over.

"Boy, it took you long enough to figure that out. I've missed you, Buddy."

And when he said that, I threw my arms around him and wept, sobbing. Laurell loved me enough to risk what I now understood to be the deepest friendship in his life as well.

*S*pring has arrived, the dawn comes earlier now, and yet I rise even before daybreak. I stand before the bathroom mirror and go through the routine of untaping the eye, donning the hairpiece, setting the plastic ear in place. Last night's service went particularly well—a large crowd in a vital church and, the essential thing, the Spirit was there with the same kind of power I remember in my father's church when I was a child; the back of my head prickled like nobody's business from the power that consecrated that meeting to the Lord's glory.

I gave my testimony, not like I have done it here; with audiences I always tell a lot of jokes, many of them *deliberately* make use of bad puns, to deflect any pity someone might feel for me. I don't want them feeling sorry for Roever; I want them feeling sorry for poor, benighted humanity, so lost in sin that the Father had to send His only Son to be crucified. I want them to see that my disfigurement is only a sign of mankind's fallen condition in which everyone shares. I want them to see it as a particularly noticeable sign of the truth of the Beatitudes, that the poor, the humble, the meek, the persecuted, and the pure in heart are the truly blessed. Unlike those who have their reward already, unlike those who love this world for its own sake, making it into an idol, the afflicted of the earth who recognize their own sinful nature will one day be healed, not of this or that particular malady but of their very mortality. And they will be made into what we were all meant to be—images of God who are privileged to be His children and share in the wealth of His glory.

And yet I cannot deny that I evoke great curiosity. Some people come just to see what I look like. Even little children knock on the door of the bus before or after the services to see the "monster man." And—what I really hate—sometimes people will come forward during an altar call, a time appointed for accepting Christ as Lord and Savior or consecrating ourselves anew to His service, and what they want is not Christ at all but my autograph. I'm trying to give them so much in the beauty and truth of Jesus—it hurts that sometimes my scars are a distraction.

The pain is still there, man, you'd better believe it. One time a fellow told me how wonderful it was that I could go on the government dole—which, as I've written, I refused to do—and live a life of leisure: To him my wounds were well worth it. Recently in a restaurant, four college kids saw me, and, as I was standing at the salad bar, they laughed at me openly and made grotesque faces which mocked my appearance. The carnal part of me wanted to tear into those people, rip that guy's lips off. But the Christ in me restrained me and helped me to see with pity the condition of their hearts that caused them to mock.

I look into the mirror today, as I go through the process of making myself more presentable, and I wonder why Jesus won't take my disfigurement from me. He healed the lepers. *Dear God, oh dear Jesus, I'd give You anything, all of my worldly goods and more, if You'd just take my disfigurement away.* As my thoughts devolve into this cry of anguish, I feel depression gathering and exhaustion setting in. I am no Samson, no Daniel, no Elijah, no John the Baptist. I have no strength to live the life that I must live today and every day until my death. And, while my day is booked solid, I have within the confines of this world, with its lure of success and power, no place to go—nothing that can get me through the day.

So, having run through the logic of this world and found in it my own emptiness, I pray the only prayer that breaks the confines of this world and opens it up to the mystery of Christ's supernatural presence. I pray, *"Be it unto me according to thy word."*

What I have endured is not directly attributable to God; Satan, as the prince of this world, inflicted my suffering for his own gratuitous delight. But the Lord can make even the evil of unmerited suffering the conduit or channel of His grace. Christ was sinless, and yet He was crucified. His was the ultimate example of unmerited suffering, but through it He became a vehicle of grace whereby all the world might be saved.

As I start the day, I try to pray as He did, *"Not my will, but thine."* Then I leave the rest of the day up to God.

Completing my morning ritual by dressing, once more I encounter my visible image in the mirror, and it reminds me of my complete dependence on the Lord. I can only acquiesce to His will, but this acquiescence opens up my life to the resurrection power of Jesus Christ. And that power *is* there. "For me to live is Christ." Jesus said, "My grace is sufficient for thee: for my grace is made perfect in weakness." God requires only one thing of us in order for Him to bring this resurrection power into our lives: He requires that we offer everything up, both those things we can control and those things beyond our control, to offer it all up so that He may redeem it. The obedience He requires is not a spotless track record; it is the determination to receive all things as from His hand, whatever their origin, so that He may make them His own. This determination will be flawed, we will sin, sin grievously sometimes against those we love the most, but if we confess our sins, He is faithful to forgive us our sins and to cleanse us from all unrighteousness. We must persevere to the end, confessing our faults, amending our lives, and thus growing in the grace and knowledge of the Lord Jesus Christ. We must strive to rest in the One who was perfectly obedient, obedient unto death, even the death of the cross.

Through the unmerited suffering of my disfigurement, my "magnificent defeat," the Lord has given me a ministry; He has made way for my vocation as an evangelist in a way He never could have otherwise. So let them come to see this freak, this monster man. *Come one, come all,* the barker might cry; *see the Human Torch who burns so brightly the night is turned into day, a man who is ever aflame and yet is not consumed! See this living miracle who is dead yet alive, whose death is his life. But stand back when he appears, stand back, ladies and gentlemen, for he longs that that same fire may burn in your own soul as well!*

At the end of my testimony I usually play the piano. My right index finger is the only one on that hand which I can move normally. The thumb is a kind of stump, the three fingers next to the index finger are permanently curled inward, and yet I have been able to teach myself how to play the piano. And I do so with all the flourish I can muster to exhibit to people that God in the consummation of all history will use everything, our limitations as well as our obedience—in fact, He will even use the plans of the Devil himself—to accomplish His final victory. He does the same thing in our lives right now, as we await the glad day when we "shall ever be with the Lord"—"to die is gain." Playing that piano fulfills the serio-comic vision I had of my new twelve-string guitar while lying on the banks of the Vam Co Tay River in Vietnam. I find this action communicates to people more than anything else the resurrection power of the Lord. *If Roever can play that piano like that with those hands,* people reason, *what undreamed-of but longed-for use might God make of my hands, my life?* I like to play the hymn whose lyrics make use of Christ's words: "I am the resurrection and the life/ he that believeth on Me *though he were dead/* yet shall he live, yet shall he live/ and whosoever liveth and believeth in Me shall never, never die."

I started out this book by saying that in a sense I have died. The Dave Roever who went to Vietnam is dead. His former appearance is gone. His Old Testament faith is gone. These things are being replaced, I pray, with the image of Christ and a love for Christ that will, through His grace, transform me into someone who can bear Christ into the world. I was a Christian before I went to Vietnam, but I had a lot to learn, and the school of charity in which I have been taught and go on learning my lessons has made me a new creation in Christ Jesus in a way impossible otherwise. I pray that He will spare you the same mercy, and I also pray that He will grant you a double portion of it. Such are His paradoxical workings.

Yet it would be false to conclude by emphasizing the victory in my life to the exclusion of the difficulties of the race which remains to be run. The apostle Paul articulated the sum of my experience when he wrote: "I am crucified with Christ: nevertheless I live; yet not I, but Christ liveth in me: and the life which I now live in the flesh I live by the faith of the Son of God, who loved me, and gave himself for me." It has been my grief and my honor to know something of the depth of those words—words that have sustained me in my darkest hours, words that allure me to hope until the day I stand before the One who gave Himself for me and I hear Him say, "Welcome home, Davey."

ABOUT THE AUTHORS

DAVE ROEVER is president of Roever Evangelistic Association, Inc.—headquartered in Ft. Worth, Texas. He travels throughout the United States and many foreign countries to hold evangelistic crusades; he produces his own weekly television program, "The Dave Roever Crusade" which airs coast to coast; and he speaks to more than 300,000 public school students each year. He also appears with Dr. Billy Graham in crusades and on national television. Rev. Roever's wife, Brenda, and their two children, Matthew and Kimberly, travel with him in his worldwide evangelistic work.

HAROLD FICKETT is a well-known author of fiction, biography, and screenplays. Among his published books are *Mrs. Sunday's Problem and Other Stories, The Holy Fool, A Modest Proposal* with Franky Schaeffer, and *Flannery O'Connor: Images of Grace*. He has also written for *The New Oxford Review, Christianity & Literature, Publishers Weekly, Christian Scholar's Review,* and *Eternity*. Currently Harold is a Fellow in the Center for Christian Writers at Friends University in Wichita, Kansas, where he lives with his wife, Mary, and their son.